MW00808198

Windows and Doors

## POETS ON POETRY

**Marilyn Hacker and Kazim Ali, Series Editors**
**Donald Hall, Founding Editor**

*New titles*

David Baker, *Show Me Your Environment*
Andrew Hudgins, *Diary of a Poem*
T. R. Hummer, *Available Surfaces*
Lawrence Joseph, *The Game Changed*
Marilyn Krysl, *Yes, There Will Be Singing*
David Mason, *Two Minds of a Western Poet*
Natasha Sajé, *Windows and Doors*
Cole Swensen, *Noise That Stays Noise*

*Recently published*

Kazim Ali, *Orange Alert*
Martín Espada, *The Lover of a Subversive Is Also a Subversive*
Annie Finch, *The Body of Poetry*
Marilyn Hacker, *Unauthorized Voices*

*Also available, collections by*

Elizabeth Alexander, Meena Alexander, A. R. Ammons, John Ashbery,
Robert Bly, Philip Booth, Marianne Boruch, Hayden Carruth,
Amy Clampitt, Alfred Corn, Douglas Crase, Robert Creeley, Donald Davie,
Thomas M. Disch, Ed Dorn, Tess Gallagher, Sandra M. Gilbert,
Dana Gioia, Linda Gregerson, Allen Grossman, Thom Gunn,
Rachel Hadas, John Haines, Donald Hall, Joy Harjo, Robert Hayden,
Edward Hirsch, Daniel Hoffman, Jonathan Holden, John Hollander,
Paul Hoover, Andrew Hudgins, Laura (Riding) Jackson,
Josephine Jacobsen, Mark Jarman, Galway Kinnell, Kenneth Koch,
John Koethe, Yusef Komunyakaa, Maxine Kumin, Martin Lammon (editor),
Philip Larkin, David Lehman, Philip Levine, Larry Levis, John Logan,
William Logan, William Matthews, William Meredith, Jane Miller,
David Mura, Carol Muske, Alice Notley, Geoffrey O'Brien, Gregory Orr,
Alicia Suskin Ostriker, Ron Padgett, Marge Piercy, Grace Schulman,
Anne Sexton, Karl Shapiro, Reginald Shepherd, Charles Simic,
William Stafford, Anne Stevenson, May Swenson, James Tate,
Richard Tillinghast, C. K. Williams, Alan Williamson, Charles Wright,
James Wright, John Yau, and Stephen Yenser

*Natasha Sajé*

# Windows and Doors

## A POET READS LITERARY THEORY

THE UNIVERSITY OF MICHIGAN PRESS

*Ann Arbor*

Published in the United States of America by
The University of Michigan Press
Manufactured in the United States of America
⊗ Printed on acid-free paper

2017   2016   2015   2014      4   3   2   1

A CIP catalog record for this book is available from the British Library.
ISBN 978-0-472-03599-1 (pbk. : alk. paper)
ISBN 978-0-472-12053-6 (e-book)

# Contents

# Preface

I started writing poetry the first time I read contemporary poetry, in seventh grade. That is when I remember thrilling to Sylvia Plath's *Ariel*. Not Shakespeare or Tennyson or Poe with their antique diction and fair ladies—rather, a woman who spoke to me and who made me want to talk back. The germ of the book you hold in your hands began, perhaps, four years after that, when the adviser of my high school literary magazine suggested an addition to one of my poems. The poem outlined the body's dissolving while the self remained. He told me to add the line "a cascade of waterfall white" to describe the melting bones. It didn't feel right, but what did I know? He was the English teacher. I added the line. When I've thought about the poem since, I shake my head. If only I could have argued that the line was frivolous: because cascade and waterfall are redundant, because "white" is clear from the previous line, and because the poem's existential point demands brevity.

Fast-forward to my first graduate school experience. During the one year (1979–1980) I did a creative writing M.A. at Johns Hopkins, I somehow ended up in a Humanities Center graduate seminar on the work of historian Michel Foucault. The room was crowded with Humanities Center students using words such as "hegemony" and "panopticon." They were speaking a foreign language, one that I had no idea how to learn. I dropped the class and added one taught by a Writing Seminars instructor. There we read and discussed twentieth-century novels. This I could do, along with writing papers about themes or close readings. I don't remember using the MLA bibliography or even library references anytime during that year.

At Hopkins back then, the writers poked fun at the theorists and their jargon and the fact that they were analyzing criticism instead of literature. I read only novels and poems that entire year. Jacques Derrida gave a talk and I didn't go.

My one-year M.A. did little to prepare me for the writing life. I'd always loved to read and write, and I'd been an English major in college, but I was driven by instinct. I had no framework for what I read and no idea how to find one. I knew what I liked, but what I liked kept changing and I couldn't explain why. For seven years after that degree, I flailed like a fish in a wide but shallow pool, attending poetry readings at the Library of Congress around the corner from the Capitol Hill restaurant where I was making a living as a waitress, reading many novels a week, and occasionally writing poems. I continued to write poems because of the economy of poetic language and its ability to convey the unsaid. I loved the silence—the white space—as much as the words. I moved back to Baltimore and taught freshman composition, and after a few years, the low adjunct pay plus a hunger to learn more drove me to Ph.D. programs in literature, first at the University of Delaware and then at the University of Maryland. Although I didn't feel confident about my poems, I thought I could write about what I read.

During my Ph.D. studies at the University of Maryland, I learned the language of that classroom at Hopkins. I felt like one of those thin, desiccated sponges dropped into water. Feminist theory allowed me to understand why I felt intimidated about speaking up in class, one insight among many. Queer theory articulated my bisexual orientation. Marxist and race theory helped me to understand the inequities I saw around me. Narrative theory explained my satisfaction (or not) with the endings of novels. Deconstruction awakened me to the push and pull of binary oppositions, including the one between poetry and prose. I was no longer a naive reader; rather, to use Robert Scholes' term, I became a crafty one. There were no poetry theorists among the faculty at Maryland, but a plethora of narrative and feminist scholars, so I wrote a dissertation that examines the coquette as a figure of discourse from Molière to Edith Wharton. I loved the reading it forced me to do, not just plays and novels and conduct books, but theory and criticism and philosophy. I let go of the notion that the only texts worth studying are formally excellent ones, as I discovered that "mistakes" and contradictions in texts could help me articulate interesting questions. And I taught sophomore-level classes in the novel, women's literature, American literature, and the English major gateway class, an introduction to theory.

I once again applied myself to writing poems, driven by the desire to document my new ways of seeing, and with the help of my women's writing group in Baltimore, I revised them. I published them in magazines. Four months after I sent it out, my first book of poems was accepted for publication. Sitting at my graduate student's desk in the "Surge Building" after I'd gotten that news, I thought maybe now someone would let me teach poetry. Yet I knew that I was still driven by instinct when writing poems, and would have difficulty justifying my choices.

When it came time to look for a full-time teaching job, I applied for creative writing jobs, since I wanted to continue to write poems. On the basis of *Red Under the Skin*, that first book of poems, I was hired to teach poetry writing part-time in the low-residency M.F.A. program at Vermont College. My first lecture was about etymology and poetry, a topic spurred by my research into the history of the word "coquette." I continued to look for a full-time job. I had many interviews, and potential colleagues often seemed suspicious. Why had I written a scholarly dissertation on the novel when I wrote poetry? Did my Ph.D. make any difference in the way I taught poetry writing? And the unspoken but palpable worry, in large departments, would I vote with the writers or the scholars? Which was I, really?

It's no wonder I ended up full-time at a small college, Westminster in Salt Lake City, where everyone in the English department had a scholarly Ph.D. and everyone taught a variety of courses. And where there was no poet on the faculty to ask me, "How would you teach John Ashbery?"—a question that, in 1995 at one campus interview, I hadn't a clue how to answer. I was beginning to understand that the poetry world was as divided as academia itself with cliques and camps. But I was also determined to bridge those camps, or rather, I couldn't help but bridge those camps simply because of my writing, reading, and teaching practices.

In one sense, this book is the answer to that question, "Does a Ph.D. make any difference in the way you teach poetry writing?" Of course, it's not the Ph.D. but the reading that makes me answer yes. I can't switch off the politically charged way I'd learned to read.

Over the years, with the help of my Westminster and Vermont College M.F.A. students and colleagues, I learned how to teach poetry writing. But when I had to recommend books for my students, I was dismayed by poetry handbooks that seemed dumbed down or frozen in the fifties. Books of essays by poets were better, but haphazard. And so much current critical writing about poetry is done in the form of book reviews or craft essays by poets who are antitheory, resisting the ideological insights I was passionate about. And finally, books by scholars of poetry (that ever-diminishing group) seemed to be speaking only to other scholars, and taking their examples from a thin slice of contemporary U.S. poetry.

*Windows and Doors* attempts to address this deficit, by placing poststructuralist and postmodern ways of thinking alongside the formalist, making explicit what is usually tacit. Each of the nine essays addresses a topic of central concern to readers and writers of poetry at the same time that it makes an original argument about poetic language and ideology. Each essay grew out of a question I initially couldn't answer. Sometimes the question changed when I discovered someone else's answer. I wrote the book I wished I had had in my poetry writing classes, first as a student and then as a teacher, one that would allow history, philosophy, and literary theory into the creative writing classroom, and one that would use truly diverse poems as examples. I wrote to a plan addressing the foundational topics of poetry: diction, syntax, rhythm, surprise, figurative language, narrative, genre, book design, and performance. I wanted to clarify the debates that are dividing poets and scholars, and write a book that is both personal and a useful teaching text, one that might, through its copious use of examples, also offer writing prompts. I wanted to write a book conveying the energy of Noble Lounge at Vermont College when I lecture there, a space of conversation and debate, a space where a poetry student who is also a surgeon can comment that the reciprocity of ethics in the operating room is akin to that of reading a poem. From their considerable expertise in fields other than poetry, I have learned much from my students. I consider these chapters provisional and hope they connect with anyone who is serious about poetry, regardless of background.

My examples are taken from what I was reading. I am sure there are better examples for every argument. Similarly, my research was somewhat haphazard, although often serendipitous, and I am sure I missed relevant and important sources for each essay. I have revised the essays for this book, but the reader should know that the essays were originally written over a fifteen-year period. I hope readers will forgive me; my aim is not to be exhaustive or authoritative but rather suggestive. My title comes from a poem by Emily Dickinson: "I dwell in Possibility / A fairer House than Prose / More numerous of Windows— / Superior—for Doors." The poem equates "possibility" with poetry, suggesting that poems have more windows and doors than prose. With these essays and these examples, I hope that I have, for some readers, opened a door to literary theory.

# Acknowledgments

Many friends, colleagues, and students have helped me think through the issues of this book. Lisa Katz was crucial to its conception and commented on most of the drafts. Linda Kauffman helped me turn the idea into a project. Madeleine Mysko made the text more coherent and readable, as did Helen Hodgson and the students in her classes. Susan Gunter graciously read the whole manuscript, and Willy Palomo helped check references. My colleagues and students at the Vermont College of Fine Arts heard these chapters as lectures, and my colleagues in the Westminster College faculty writing group commented on chapter drafts. All of their suggestions were invaluable.

In addition, for critical insights and feedback, I thank Lisa Bickmore, Jean Cheney, Gerry Connolly, Karen Garthe, Mark Halliday, David Hamilton, Andrea Hollander, Kimberly Johnson, Lance Larsen, Laura Ann Manning, Seth Michaelson, Paisley Rekdal, Susan Sample, Anita Sherman, Elaine Terranova, and Jennifer Tonge. Thanks also to the many people who wrote to me when chapters were published in their first versions.

Important institutional support was given by the Utah Humanities Council, Westminster College, the Camargo Foundation, and a Fulbright grant to Slovenia. I am grateful also to the editors and staff of the journals in which some of these essays first appeared. Versions of the first through fourth, sixth, and seventh essays were published in *The Writer's Chronicle*; a version of the first essay appeared in *The American Poetry Review*; and a version of the eighth appeared in *The Iowa Review*. Finally, I offer thanks to the staff and editors of the University of Michigan Press, particularly Kazim Ali and Marilyn Hacker (who chose the manuscript), and Susan Cronin and Aaron McCollough, who saw it through the publishing process with enthusiasm and acumen.

# Roots in Our Throats

## A Case for Using Etymology

Every piece of writing depends on two language tools—diction and syntax—tools so basic that writers often don't think about them. But poets in particular need to pay attention to syntax and diction. While the teller of a story may successfully employ very simple syntax and diction—as in the folktale—the poet is ever intent on refining these tools, even in the seemingly simplest of poems. Samuel Taylor Coleridge, in *Table Talk*, July 12, 1827, says as much: "I wish our clever young poets would remember my homely definitions of prose and poetry; that is, prose = words in their best order; poetry = the best words in their best order."

Our focus, then, begins with diction—the deliberate choosing of the "best" words. An understanding of diction is rooted in understanding the very origin of those words, that is, with etymology. Because English words have origins in Anglo-Saxon, Latin, and Greek, a writer can often choose between these "families" to achieve a particular effect. Moreover, understanding etymology allows a writer to tap into buried or historical meanings of words, thereby amplifying the effect of a single image. And finally, etymology provides access to history and an understanding of ideological change.

Because language changes more slowly than culture, etymology reveals surprising disparities between the two. The word "malaria," for example, comes from the Italian ("bad air"). When the word was coined, the disease was thought to be caused by the air around Roman swamps, but we now know the disease is caused by mosquitoes carrying protozoa. The word "pride," for another example, referred to the "first sin" during Milton's era, but today "pride" connotes a badge of honor, as in "gay pride."

In the case of "pride," a change in context appears to have risen from a change in thinking about individual power. Thus a contemporary American reader might consider Adam's "pride" ("man's first disobedience") as a positive attribute, akin to taking initiative. Etymology, we see, is the tool that helps writers to understand their cultures.

My personal understanding of etymology and the ideological nature of language has been shaped by philosophy, specifically by the work of Friedrich Nietzsche, Martin Heidegger, Ludwig Wittgenstein, and Jacques Derrida. In his essay "Building, Thinking, Dwelling," Heidegger writes that language "tells us about the nature of a thing, provided that we respect language's own nature. In the meantime, to be sure, there rages round the earth an unbridled yet clever talking, writing, and broadcasting of spoken words. Man acts as though he were the shaper and master of language, while in fact language remains the master of man."[1] Language represents ideology, a web of assumptions about the world, a web too large and powerful for any one person to change. In this respect, language supports the status quo, the best example being the case of English, a language that represents a patriarchal ideology. And so by providing access to ideology, language helps us understand problems in the status quo.

### Families of Words

The English language is lexically rich because of its history. From Old Norse influence we get basic words such as "she" and "they," plus everyday nouns like "skin" and "egg." When the Norman French invaded England in 1066, French became the language of the English court and the ruling class, and Germanic-based Old English was relegated to "the common people." For a period of four hundred years, English both lost distinct letters and gained new spellings from the French. By Shakespeare's time, English had also absorbed many Latin and Greek words. By the time Samuel Johnson wrote his dictionary in 1755, the challenge was to standardize what had already become an unruly—or gloriously rich—language, infused with new words prompted by colonization, exploration, and technology. Meanwhile, as English entered the New World, it was further enriched by Native American words (such as "canoe" and "moccasin") and borrowings fueled by British colonialism, such as "dinghy" and "pajamas" from Hindi. Like French, German, and Italian, the English language has Indo-European roots, but English diction is less pure—and more interesting—because its synonyms have roots in both the Anglo-Saxon and the Latinate/Greek, and because it has also absorbed "New World" words.

Until our era, most writers learned Latin and Greek. They were trained, too, in the history and structure of English, and in etymology. Even William Blake, who was not trained in classical languages, taught himself enough about Latin and Greek to use the devices of etymology in his poems. Times have changed, however. While a good portion of high school students do study a foreign language, we know that only a fraction of them (about 1 percent) study Latin, and still fewer study Greek.[2] Fewer still have exposure to the history of English. This means that most contemporary readers and writers must make a conscious effort to learn etymology by looking up words in a dictionary that lists word roots.

That conscious effort pays off for the writer who chooses words with an eye (and ear) to their history. Consider, for example, the word *inculcate*, which is sometimes used as a synonym for *teach*. The root of *inculcate* is the Latin word for *heel* (*calx*), and so when it is used as a synonym for *teach* it bears within it that image of a heel pressing something into the ground, and its metaphorical meaning is colored by that violence. The first listing for *inculcate* in the Oxford English Dictionary is a 1550 use by Coverdale: "This practyse dyd the holy elect of god in the olde time not onli inculcate and teach with words but also expresse and performe in dede."

Like Coverdale, contemporary writers can choose words from one or both families of our language. For example, the Anglo-Saxon word *woods* suggests something different from the Latinate *forest*, even though the two are equivalents. Imagine the Latinate version of Frost's poem, "Stopping by the [Forest] on a Snowy Evening": "whose [forest] this is I think I know." Furthermore, the Anglo-Saxon branch of our language is a boon to poets in particular because of its many monosyllabic words, which are easier to work with in metrical verse.

Below is a list of some Anglo-Saxon words alongside Latinate or Greek "equivalents":

| | |
|---|---|
| fear | phobia |
| truth | veracity |
| mad | insane |
| lazy | indolent |
| fat | obese |
| woods | forest |
| shit | excrement |
| worry | uneasiness, anxiety |
| speak | discourse |
| dark | obscure |
| greedy | rapacious |
| short | insufficient |
| light | illumination |
| fire | conflagration |
| eat | consume |
| weird | idiosyncratic |
| sorrow | anguish, melancholy |
| green | verdant |
| skin | epidermis |
| chew | masticate |
| heart | cardio |
| water | aqua |
| first | primary |
| horse | equine |
| thrill | ecstasy |
| fair | equitable |
| will | testament |

Football coaches would be more likely to use Anglo-Saxon diction. Bureaucrats load up Latinate diction because—pun intended—it obfuscates. And lawyers, who have a tendency to play it safe when conveying ideas, often use both at the same time, as we see in the last two entries in the above list.

Writers in English may choose between Anglo-Saxon words that are more of the gut and the body, and Latinate or Greek words that seem, at least to an American ear, to be more of the head and therefore more intellectual. A native speaker of Italian once pointed out to me that, to her ear, Latinate words actually sounded more natural and body-centered, and so it seems that even *within* cultures, people may hear words idiosyncratically, based on regional, family, and bodily differences. But these differences are subtle. In the end, English is a dance between the Anglo-Saxon and the Latinate/Greek.

Some writers do tend more toward one or the other. Look, for example, at these two-second sentences from stories by Henry James and Raymond Carver:

1. The pair of mourners, sufficiently stricken, were in the garden of the vicarage together, before luncheon, waiting to be summoned to that meal, and Arthur Prime had still in his face the intention, she was moved to call it the expression, of feeling something or other.[3]
2. The four of us were sitting around his kitchen table drinking gin.[4]

James and Carver set up their stories in an identical journalistic fashion, laying out who's doing what, and when and how. But James is more inclined toward Latinate/Greek words, while Carver, with his spare sentences, is more inclined toward Anglo-Saxon. Neither inclination should come as a surprise, given that we know on the one hand of James' concern with consciousness and his distaste for the body's grossness, and on the other of Carver's pride in his working-class roots. Most writers tend not to be so clearly inclined toward the one or the other. In fact, art depends on balancing the two, using an Anglo-Saxon word when it might carry more weight or fit the meter and using the Latinate word when it might surprise or suggest a shift of thought—or fit a different meter.

Look at what happens when the poet Josephine Jacobsen purposefully restricts herself to Anglo-Saxon diction:

*The Monosyllable*

One day
she fell
in love with its
heft and speed.
Tough, lean,

fast as light
slow
as a cloud.
It took care
of rain, short

noon, long dark.
It had rough kin;
did not stall.
With it, she said,
I may,

if I can,
sleep; since I must
die.
Some say,
rise.[5]

I often refer to this poem when I teach diction. I ask my students
to "mess up" Jacobsen's poem by substituting Latinate or Greek
words for her monosyllables. The results are often hilarious and
always instructive. The word *die*, for example, has a different con-
notation and sound than *terminate* or *expire*. The word *rise* is very
different from *ascend*. Anglo-Saxon diction, as Jacobsen demon-
strates, does indeed have "heft and speed." Moreover, using it
exclusively in a poem like this dictates a shorter line. Imagine
the poem with pentameter lines: "One day she fell in love with
its heft and speed." Because the monosyllables are more concen-
trated, because they pack more meaning into the line, the reader
needs white space surrounding them in order to have time to
absorb them. If the monosyllable were not Jacobsen's point, a
Latinate word or two might actually provide merciful relief.

A telling fact to keep in mind: 60 percent of English words

have Latin roots, but if we narrow the search to English words that contain more than two syllables, we find that 90 percent of those words come from Latin.[6]

## Embedded Meanings

The etymology of a word can deepen the meaning of a poem by carrying an image, as in the poem below by Madeleine Mysko. See if you can guess which word carries an important image here.

*Out of Blue*

It wasn't wind or thunder; color foretold
A summer storm. The orange tiger lily,
The yellow black-eyed Susan, the pink phlox
Were too much themselves in the charged light.
The trees to the west sharpened against the sky.
The sky was exaggerated, a purple hue.

I set out to gather toys from the yard
And towels from the line, but at the hedge was struck
By hydrangea blue. I felt it travel,
Through me, toward the ground of a day
I couldn't quite remember, and I was left
Bewildered, bereft of I didn't know what.

I had to lean into the broad leaves, to reach
Deep, to snap stems until my arms
Were filled with blooms as big as baby bonnets.
The broken-green odor blessed the air
As I carried that crucial blue across the lawn,
And the maples blanched at the first gust of wind.[7]

The poem tells the story of a woman who goes into her yard to gather toys before a summer storm. "Bewildered, bereft," she snaps some hydrangea blossoms to carry back into the house, and is consoled. The color of the flowers is "crucial blue." The word *crucial* comes from the Latin *crux* ("cross"). Of course a reader can understand the poem without the etymology of *cru-*

*cial,* but the reader who sees the image of the woman carrying the blossoms as a suggestion of Christ carrying the cross, reads "Out of Blue" more clearly as a poem of faith and redemption.

Paisley Rekdal's "Stupid"[8] also contains embedded etymological meaning. The poem refers to the Darwin Awards, which commemorate "those who improve our gene pool by removing themselves from it in really stupid ways."[9] The poem relates several Darwin Award stories, including those of one man who drowned in two feet of water and a second man who was stabbed to death by a friend while trying to prove a knife couldn't penetrate a flak vest. Rekdal has braided these instances of human stupidity along with the story of Job, "that book of the pious man/ who suffered because the devil wanted to teach God / faith kills through illusion." Toward the end of the poem Job is directly addressed: "Job, you are stupid for your faith as we are stupid for our lack of it, / snickering at the stockbrocker jogging off the cliff, though / shouldn't we wonder at all a man can endure/ to believe."

The etymology of *stupid,* which doesn't actually appear in the body of the poem, deepens its meaning. The word *stupid* comes from the Latin *stupere* ("to be astonished"), which comes from the Greek *typein* ("to beat")—the root of our words *stupefy* and *stupendous.* Rekdal's "Stupid" considers the borders between faith and insanity, joy and despair, life and death. The image of a person being astonished (the origin of "stupid") affects how the reader evaluates the behavior discussed. Consequently, in the poem, winners of the Darwin Award—like Job—seem to be acting on faith rather than merely exercising poor judgment.

Examples of embedded etymological meanings are abundant in the works of Chaucer, Shakespeare, and Milton. Thanks to his knowledge of roots, prefixes, and suffixes, Milton coined many words, including "pandemonium," "disfigurement," and "displode." The prefix "dis," Neil Forsyth tells us, is related to the Greek *dis,* "but picks up the flavor of the Greek prefix 'dys,' meaning unlucky or ill."[10] "Dis" is also the name of the inner city and principal inhabitant of Dante's Hell. This understanding gives the first line of *Paradise Lost* ("Of man's first disobedience and the fruit") deeper significance. The writer who uses etymology draws upon deep resources. The reader who understands this web of etymological connections has a richer experience than one who does not.

Ralph Waldo Emerson's much-quoted line—"Language is fossil poetry," from his essay "The Poet"—speaks to his understanding of the primacy of etymology. Emerson argues that the poet's power comes from his ability to use the archetypal symbols that are words. The poet, Emerson says, is "the Namer, or Language-maker" and the etymologist "finds the deadest word to have been once a brilliant picture."[11] Walt Whitman also championed the use of etymology, arguing that "the scope of [English] etymologies is the scope not only of man and civilization, but the history of Nature in all departments, and of the organic Universe, brought up to date; for all are comprehended in words, and their backgrounds."[12] In discussing Whitman's project, Joseph Kronick goes as far as to argue that it "will be to refashion the language through an etymological uncovering of origins. This presumptive historical task will, however, be conducted on common speech, American slang to be precise, rather than within the Indo-European family of languages."[13]

Gerard Manley Hopkins is a poet whose interest in etymology is well documented in his diaries. For instance, the entry for September 24, 1863, is an etymological riff on the word "horn":

> The various lights under which a horn may be looked at have given rise to a vast number of words in language. It may be regarded as a projection, a climax, a badge of strength, power or vigour, a tapering body, a spiral, a wavy object, a bow, a vessel to hold withal or to drink from, a smooth hard material not brittle, stony, metallic or wooden, something sprouting up, something to thrust or push with, a sign of honour or pride, an instrument of music, etc. From the shape, *kernel* and *granum, grain, corn*. From the curve of the horn, κορωνις, *corona, crown*. From the spiral *crinis*, meaning ringlets, locks. From its being the highest point comes our crown perhaps, in the sense of the top of the head, and the Greek κέρας, horn, and κάρα, head, were evidently identical; then for its sprouting up and growing, compare *keren, cornu*, κέρας, horn with grow, *cresco, grandis*, grass, great, *groot*.[14]

The above passage is only half the entry, but we can see Hopkins' mind ranging over the word and its histories, even inventing etymology as a way of combining images with history.

In the hands of a skilled etymologist, such riffs become ways to think about cultural and historical change, as when Martin Heidegger follows the etymologies of the German *bauen* ("build"), which originally meant "to dwell," or "to stay in a place":

> The real meaning of the verb *bauen* has been lost to us. But a cover trace of it has been preserved in the German word, *Nachbar*, neighbor. The neighbor is in Old English the *neahgebur; neah*, near, and *gebur*, dweller. The *Nachbar* is the *Nachgebur*, the *Nachgebauer*, the near-dweller, he who dwells nearby. . . . The way in which you and I am, the manner in which we humans are on the earth, is *Buan*, dwelling. To be a human being means to be on the earth as a mortal. It means to dwell. The old word *bauen*, which says that man *is* insofar as he dwells, this word *bauen* however also means at the same time to cherish and protect, specifically to till the soil, to cultivate the vine.[15]

At a time when building usually means ruining the earth by imposing our will on it, Heidegger reminds us how we have drifted from the notion of "cherish and protect."

A contemporary American novelist passionate about etymology is Paul West, whose book *The Secret Lives of Words* is a personal and entertaining etymological dictionary. West admits that he began a novel about astronomy with the word *consider*, which means "set alongside the stars" from the prefix *cum* ("with") and *sidus* ("star"). West notes that ancient astrologers coined this word fixed on the stars, and yet more recent astrologers are actually fixed on planets. "Tracking the courses of stars," West continues, "soon weakened into observing them, and that into observing in general, and in no time observing has become 'remarking,' not in the sense of 'notice' but in that of 'saying,' in which case it joins the abominable modern 'I was' and 'I went,' both referring to speech."[16] West's book, like Hopkins' diary entries, testifies to the addictive nature of learning etymologies. Every unknown word is a mystery waiting to be solved.

# False Etymologies

Even incorrect or "false" etymologies can provide material for poems. Susan Mitchell's poem "The False Etymologies of Isidore of Seville"[17] tells the story of Isidore (AD 560–636), the Christian bishop and scholar who produced *Etymologiae*, or *Origines*, as it is sometimes called. Enormously popular throughout the Middle Ages, Isidore's work attempted to compile all knowledge in an encyclopedic fashion. Isidore's quest points to a recurrent theme in etymology, that of the search for origins *and* universal truth. In Mitchell's poem Isidore of Seville believes in "This one / from that, eyrie from air, so ear from airy, the ear / a nest that hears in air its own name." But then the poet admits that she's "translating," that she's "making this up." However, if Mitchell invents the particulars, the gist remains: Isidore's desire to understand origins led him to make erroneous connections on his religious journey:

He wants to follow the initial S for Salvation,
pursue the long curve of the swan's
song back up to the winding
throat and dab the first fruit with his own saliva.

He'll do it on hands and knees, the pilgrimage
of each word to its source, first sound
from which the others
bubbled up, original gurgling innocent of sense.

Mitchell's poem suggests that the poet's interest in language is rooted (pun intended) in a different religion, that of pleasure: "I haven't his patience. I haven't got / all eternity. I skip to the parts I love best, the vowels / steeped like peaches in brandy." The poem ends by stating that the language of pleasure is childish, but also that pleasure is as powerful a motivation as scholarship:

The language of pleasure is makeshift, leaves and branches
hastily thrown. Of mud and dribble.
Of huff and puff and higgledy-piggledy.
Of rampage, ruckus. Of blow your house down.

If "true etymology" reveals history, then "false etymology" reveals wishful thinking, the connections we make in our effort to order the world. Often the reach for the "essential truth" of etymology rises from religious faith, which in English speakers reaches toward Christianity. Gjertrud Schnackenberg's poem "Supernatural Love"[18] gives us another vision of the "dictionary mystic" and the search for truth, focusing on the etymology of the word *carnation*, whose root is the Latin *carne* ("flesh"). While the speaker's father "bends to pore / over the Latin blossom" of words, his four-year-old daughter is trying to needlepoint. The little girl refers to carnations as "Christ's flowers," which prompts the father to look up the word *clove* (the scent of the flower) and he finds "from French, for clou, meaning a nail." Thus in "Supernatural Love," the child makes an etymological link that produces a mystical (but false, as the carnation takes its name from the color that the flower shares with blood) truth:

> The incarnation blossoms, flesh and nail,
> I twist my threads like stems into a knot
> And smooth "Beloved," but my needle caught
> Within the threads, *Thy blood so dearly bought,*
> The needle strikes my finger to the bone.

Other examples of poets who create false etymologies to think through problems include poets as disparate as Elizabeth Alexander and Allen Grossman. In Elizabeth Alexander's "Affirmative Action Blues,"[19] the speaker implores her boss not to use the word "niggardly" even though its etymology, she admits, is "probably / derived from French Norman, and that Chaucer and Milton and / Shakespeare used it. It means 'stingy,' and the root is not the same as 'nigger,' / which derives from 'negar,' meaning black, but they are, perhaps, / perhaps, etymologically related. The two 'g's' are two teeth gnawing, / rodent is from the Latin 'rodere' which means 'to gnaw.'" The poet is replicating the kind of leap that is common in a false etymology—a leap that makes sense even if it isn't accurate.

Allen Grossman's "Sentinel Yellowwoods"[20] is a kind of ode to the yellowwood tree, *cladrastis lutea.* The root *lutea* comes from the Latin word meaning "yellow," while the word for the instrument—the lute—comes from German and Arab roots that contain no reference to color. Grossman riffs on "odorous silent adorning lutes," synesthetically combining the sight, scent, and sound of the trees into an intimation of his own mortality: "I am going to die soon, and their shadow foretells it/ enlarging the world." That Grossman knows he is creating a false link is apparent from his reference to "flowers Arabian, and blazing with gladdening metals / Mysterious flies."


## Historical Impact

We have seen that, true or false, etymology in poems becomes a way to access ideology—a way to access assumptions about what is normal in our culture. Word histories actually provide a means to trace the evolution (or devolution) in our thinking. Note that the word "etymology" itself comes from the Greek *eteos*, meaning "true." Understanding word origins is a way of understanding history, and more specifically understanding how context changes meaning. For much of the twentieth century, formalism (or New Criticism) reigned supreme, and critics examined literary texts divorced from their context. Now literary criticism has once again begun to appreciate—and even to rely on—contexts. Poststructuralist criticism often focuses on such contextual issues as history, gender, race, and sexual orientation. Even when a poststructuralist critic focuses solely on the text, it is to look for slippages, gray areas, and the non-sense of the thing—what is sometimes termed a "Derridean reading," or deconstruction. Poststructuralists insist that etymology is important not as a search for fixed origins, but rather as a search for determinations.

Because narrative lends itself to contextual study, it comes as no surprise that more exciting theoretical work is being done on narrative. For example, a New Historicist might look at colonial American medical records in order to understand the high rate of premarital pregnancy in eighteenth-century America—an understanding that affects the reading of novels written at that time. But lyric poetry, which takes its essence from human universality, does not lend itself as easily to New Historical criticism.

Sappho's poems, for example, speak to us two thousand years after their writing because of the primacy of desire—a speaker who wants her love object to see her:

> He's a god, that man who sits with you, who listens to you talk and laugh. Seeing you with him makes my heart pound, and because you are lost to me, I can't speak, my tongue breaks into pieces, and fire runs under my skin. I'm blinded, my ears ring, sweat pours down, and my body trembles. Paler than summer wheat, I might as well be dead.[21]

No wonder that Sappho is more popular today than a poet like Dryden, whose poems require so much understanding of context. History is interested in the unique, in things that happen once and only once, or the relationship of the singular to the cyclical, while lyric poetry focuses on the repeated feeling, on a timeless evocation of the human condition, particularly human emotion. But this is not to say that etymology is of no use to the lyric poet. On the contrary, etymology provides the lyric poet a useful access to history, just as it provides the reader of lyric poetry a way to read more contextually.

While Isidore of Seville saw etymology as a path to concrete origins and lasting truth, later philosophers have been chipping away at these ideas. Nietzsche writes, "Woman (truth) will not be pinned down."[22] Jacques Derrida elaborates on the analogy, pointing to the positive aspects of truth that is not fixed. Derrida argues that Nietzsche understood that women (like Jews) are artists and masters of style, and that style (the superficial) is a more useful way to think about truth than permanent core or centrality. Truth is transient, contextual, shifting; it is not behind a veil, *it is* the veil, according to Jacques Derrida—not something to be uncovered, but rather contained only in movement.[23]

Derrida is one of the more recent philosophers who, over the last two hundred years, have gradually moved to this understanding of truth. They have abandoned the notion of Descartes, for example, that truth could be arrived at through reason, and that once arrived at, it would remain fixed. The Enlightenment confidence in rationality and definitive science has been challenged on this and on many other fronts, as when, for example, philosopher Ludwig Wittgenstein stressed language as truth's unstable "carrier." Language then—and by extension etymology, the unfolding meanings of a word—is not a vehicle for direct and final meaning (*logocentrism*) but is instead the medium on which constellations of power actually shape the true and the false. Etymology becomes a means to analyze these wrestling discourses. Truth changes according to context.

Quite a few contemporary poets—Angie Estes, David Gewanter, Kevin McFadden, Campbell McGrath, and Harryette Mullen come to mind—make etymology their explicit subject for poems, offering occasions for thinking about contexts, history, and shifting truth. Etymology is also a resource I counsel students to use when they are stuck; I tell them to open the dictionary to a word or word history they don't know and put it in a poem. The key to this exercise is the initial state of inquiry that sends the poet on a journey of discovery. The poet doesn't know what the poem, finally, will be "about" when he uses the word's etymology as a starting point before he knows the twists and turns of its history. For example, when I decided to write about vanilla as part of a series of poems about food, I researched its etymology, discovering that it comes from the Spanish *vainilla*, diminutive of the Latin *vagina* ("sheath"). Thus, the pod-shaped bean was named after the vagina, which itself was named for the function it provides for the penis. This seems to me to be the quintessential demonstration of patriarchal language, a demonstration that might seem shocking, as it seemed to have been when one magazine editor (to whom I submitted the resulting poem) asked if the ending—"no matter that some words glide over the tongue, / entice us with sweet stories, / we're still stuck / with their roots in our throats"[24]—were a reference to *Deep Throat*. Had we continued our dialogue, I would have said yes, in the sense that women are dominated by the patriarchal nature of language in the same way that Linda Lovelace was dominated.

Did Heather McHugh know that her poem would take the shape of a "dirge" when she started looking up the string of words in the poem below?

*Etymological Dirge*

> *'Twas grace that taught my heart to fear . . .*

Calm comes from burning.
Tall comes from fast.
Comely doesn't come from come.
Person comes from mask.

The kin of charity is whore,
the root of charity is dear.
Incentive has its source in song
and winning in the sufferer.

Afford yourself what you can carry out.
A coward and a coda share a word.
We get our ugliness from fear.
We get our danger from the lord.[25]

In Gary Snyder's "Earrings Dangling and Miles of Desert," the etymology of a plant name broadens the scope and shows human relations to the natural world.[26] The poem takes shape as an extended definition of sagebrush—artemesia, the plant that grows over vast stretches of the American West and is rapidly being choked out by nonindigenous and faster growing annuals such as cheatgrass. Combining prose and poetry, Snyder tells us the growing habits and uses of sagebrush, as well as its variations around the world, including mugwort and moxa in China. He also gives artemisia's Paiute names. He ends the poem with a lyric ode:

> Artem in Greek meant "to dangle" or "earring"
> (Well-connected, "articulate," art. . . .)
> Her blue-gray-green
> stretching out there
> sagebrush flats reach to the edge
> bend away—
> emptiness far as the mind can see—
> Raincloud maidens come walking

lightning-streak silver,<br>
gray skirts sweeping and trailing—

> *Hail, Artemisia,*
>> *aromatic in the rain,*
>>> *I will think of you in my other poems.*

Ultimately, Snyder uses etymology to create the image of the earrings, the title for his poem, and as a way of "humanizing" a plant whose destiny concerns him.

Etymology becomes a way of thinking about what is—and more importantly—what is possible. Through etymology, writers have the power to understand how ideology works, and perhaps even to tug its tail. Understanding what is and why it is permits us slowly, incrementally, to change. The writer who uses etymology, implicitly or explicitly, accesses not only the history of words, but of ideas.

*Notes*

1. Martin Heidegger, *Poetry, Language, Thought,* trans. Albert Hofstadter (New York: Harper & Row, 1971), 146.

2. Conrad Barrett, "Keys to Language and Cultural Awareness," *Bolchazy-Carducci Publishers,* August 31, 2012, http://www.bolchazy.com/al/keys.htm.

3. Henry James, "Paste," in *The Story and Its Writer,* ed. Ann Charters (New York: St. Martin's, 1999).

4. Raymond Carver, "What We Talk about When We Talk about Love," in Charters, *Story and Its Writer.*

5. Josephine Jacobsen, *Chinese Insomniacs* (Philadelphia: University of Pennsylvania Press, 1981), 51. Reprinted with permission of the University of Pennsylvania Press.

6. Barrett, "Keys to Language."

7. Madeleine Mysko, "Out of Blue," *Hudson Review* 47, no. 1 (Spring 1994), 80. Reprinted with permission of the author.

8. Paisley Rekdal, "Stupid," in *Six Girls Without Pants: Poems* (Spokane: Eastern Washington University Press), 1–9.

9. Darwin Awards, May 1, 2003, www.darwinawards.com.

10. Neil Forsyth, "Of Man's First Dis," in *Milton in Italy: Contexts, Im-*

*ages, Contradictions,* ed. Mario A. Di Cesare (Binghamton, NY: Medieval & Renaissance Texts and Studies, 1981).

11. Ralph Waldo Emerson, *Essays and Lectures* (New York: Library of America, 1983), 457.

12. Walt Whitman, *Prose Works 1892: Specimen Days,* ed. Floyd Stovall (New York: NYU Press, 1963), 2:572.

13. Joseph Kronick, "On the Border of History: Whitman and the American Sublime," in *The American Sublime* (Albany: SUNY Press, 1986), 59.

14. Gerard Manley Hopkins, *The Journals and Papers of Gerard Manley Hopkins,* ed. Humphrey House (Oxford: Oxford University Press, 1959), 4.

15. Heidegger, *Poetry, Language, Thought.*

16. Paul West, *The Secret Lives of Words* (New York: Harcourt, 2000), 69.

17. Susan Mitchell, *Rapture* (New York: HarperCollins, 1992), 74.

18. Gjertrud Schnackenberg, *The Lamplit Answer* (New York: Farrar, Straus & Giroux, 1985), 81–83.

19. Elizabeth Alexander, *Body of Life* (Chicago: Tia Chucha Press, 1996), 58–59.

20. Allen Grossman, *Of the Great House: A Book of Poems* (New York: New Directions, 1982), 52–53.

21. My translation.

22. Cited in Jacques Derrida, *Spurs,* trans. Barbara Harlow (University of Chicago Press, 1979), 55.

23. Derrida, *Spurs,* 59–60.

24. Natasha Sajé, *Red Under the Skin* (Pittsburgh: University of Pittsburgh Press, 1994), 7.

25. Heather McHugh, *The Father of the Predicaments* (Middletown: Wesleyan University Press, 1999), 77. Reprinted with permission of Wesleyan University Press.

26. Gary Snyder, *Mountains and Rivers Without End* (Washington, DC: Counterpoint, 1996), 125–27.

# Front-Loading Syntax

*As I altered my syntax, I altered my intellect.*
W. B. Yeats

While animals communicate using signals that refer to whole
situations, syntax is unique to human beings. Animal calls (bird-
song, for example) can be continuous analogue signals or a se-
ries of random variations one a time, but my cat's meow while
standing in front of his empty food bowl differs from Oliver
Twist's "Please, sir, I want some more." Oliver can separate the
parts of his sentence to form new ones. In other words, human
language consists of components that have their own meaning
and can be arranged to make new messages. Syntax allows for
a larger language repertoire and bypasses mere memorization.
Humans memorize words and their functions (for example,
whether they are nouns or verbs) but they do not memorize ev-
ery message they relate.

Thirty years ago linguist Noam Chomsky argued that human
babies are born with a sense of syntax that transcends individual
languages. Since then, others have been attempting to discover
universal patterns. For instance, Gugliemo Cinque posits that
every language consists of sentences based on a verb phrase sur-
rounded by modifiers in predictable patterns.[1] When the field
narrows to a particular language, patterns become easy to iden-
tify (grammatical rules). In order to write well, writers must mas-
ter not only words, but also syntax, the rules of their ordering.
Moreover, understanding syntax allows writers to bend or break
rules in ways that serve their work.

# Form and Content

Syntax reveals the interrelatedness of form and content, and the paradoxes that result in discussing one without the other. Most literature contains paraphrasable ideas; its form (including syntax) conveys these ideas. In *The Rhetoric*, Aristotle writes:

> For it is not enough to know *what* we ought to say; we must also say it *as* we ought. . . . The arts of language cannot help but having a small but real importance . . . the way in which a thing is said does affect its intelligibility. Not however, so much importance as people think. All such arts are fanciful and meant to charm the hearer. Nobody uses fine language when teaching geometry.[2]

Using the model of an orator convincing a crowd, Aristotle seems to separate form and content, yet Martha Nussbaum argues that in ancient Greece "forms of writing were not seen as vessels into which different contents could be indifferently poured; form was itself a statement, a content."[3] The answer to the apparent contradiction rests in flexible use of the terms "form" and "content." Any attempt to impose a neat or chronological development of the relationship of form to content has been, at least for me, impossible. Form and content are variables on a seesaw that can be tipped in either direction.

Suspicion of "fine language," for instance, stretches from the Bible and Aristotle to contemporary anthropologist Yi-Fu Tuan, who believes that "truth dwells, if anywhere, in simple speech. Christ said: 'plain yes or no is all you need to say; anything beyond that comes from the devil' . . . truth cannot be netted in artful speech."[4] If style is like a dress that adorns a body, an attack on style is a quick way to discredit a writer. For instance, John Locke in *An Essay Concerning Human Understanding* associates rhetoric with "the Fair Sex": "All the Art of Rhetorick, besides Order and Clearness, all the artificial and figurative application of Words Eloquence hath invented, are for nothing else but to insinuate wrong Ideas, move the Passions, and thereby mislead the Judgment . . . Eloquence, like the Fair Sex has too prevailing Beauties in it, to suffer itself ever to be spoken against."[5] We

might note the other binary oppositions alluded to here: male/
female, reason/emotion, mind/body. Seeing that "eloquence"
and the "fair sex" were equated in order to dismiss them, some
women writers rejected "flowery diction" and "elegant" syntax.
Here, for example, is Mary Wollstonecraft:

> Wishing rather to persuade by the force of my arguments,
> than dazzle by the elegance of my language, I shall not waste
> my time rounding periods, or in fabricating the turgid bom-
> bast of artificial feelings. . . . I shall be employed about things,
> not words![6]

Wollstonecraft's division between style and content is termed
*dualism*. Dualists believe there are different ways of saying the
same thing, that a sentence can be paraphrased and not lose
its message. In 1818 Hegel addressed the relation of form to
content in his Heidelberg lectures on aesthetics, dividing works
of art into three categories: symbolic, classic, and romantic. Sym-
bolic art, such as the "oriental," "vainly endeavors to find pure
conceptions and a mode of representation which is suitable to
them. It is a conflict between matter and form, both imperfect
and heterogeneous."[7] Classic art, such as sculpture, unites form
and content in harmony. Romantic art emphasizes form over
content, so that form becomes its truth—and poetry is the art
which unites form and content: "Poetry is the universal art of the
mind which has become free in its own nature, and which has
not tried to find its realization in external sensuous matter, but
expatiates exclusively in the inner space and inner time of the
ideas and feelings."[8]

Dante wrote, "The exposition of the letter is nothing other
than the development of the form,"[9] but these ideas really blos-
somed in nineteenth- and twentieth-century thinking. It is the
form that makes art, insisted Flaubert, Tolstoy, and the New Crit-
ics, taking the stance called *monism*, which finds form and con-
tent inseparable, and believes that any change in style results in
a change of meaning. Monists see a text as a whole, and to take
this view to the extreme would be to say that meaning can only
be expressed by repeating the very words of the original text.
This recalls the medieval form of monism, the icon, wherein

form and content are so inseparable as to be endowed with one (holy) spirit. Indeed, for some twenty-first-century artists, art is the new icon, with the artist a stand-in for God.

Yet for others art is only surfaces, without content or "depth"— even without a controlling human consciousness. Fredric Jameson notes the poststructuralist repudiation of philosophical, psychological, and linguistic "depth models," arguing that "depth is replaced by surface or by multiple surfaces."[10] Such binary oppositions between form and content, truth and falsehood, and natural and artificial led twentieth-century philosopher Jacques Derrida to challenge "the good and the natural [as] the divine inscription in the heart and the soul; the perverse and the artful [as] technique, exiled in the exteriority of the body."[11] These ongoing tensions between truth and art are reflected in discussions of syntax.

In a 1959 letter to Elaine Feinstein, Charles Olson expresses a monist view when he writes "that form is never any more than an extension of content."[12] Not all modern poets are monists, however. In "Against Decoration," her afterword to *Viper Rum*, Mary Karr cites poems by Amy Clampitt and James Merrill, among others, that spend their energy on "surfaces." Karr argues that when "decorative elements" become "final ends," the poems fail to move the reader."[13] She advocates art that emphasizes the artist's expression of emotion as a conduit for the reader's. She cites Merrill's "Serenade" as a poem whose "flourishes . . . obscure the central subject, render it meaningless."[14] But one could argue that although "Serenade" may not be one of Merrill's best poems, neither is it meaningless. One could also argue that the situation of past lovers reduced to corresponding with each other, one by letter, the other by poem, is clear; that the emotions described are longing, anticipation, and loyalty; and that the art of both the letter and the poem become light by which to see. My point is that some readers use the complaint of artifice to dismiss writing they don't like.

*Pluralism* offers a third approach that tries to avoid the weaknesses of monism and dualism in their respective denial of content and form. Geoffrey Leech and Michael Short propose a pluralist model that incorporates three levels of style: semantic, syntactic, and graphological. On the semantic level (that of message), the pluralist would consider "the discreet door closed with a click" and "the door discreetly shut with a click" to transmit the "same" message, despite slight differences in meaning.[15] On the syntactic level "the discreet door shut with a click" and "with a click the discreet door shut" have different effects but transmit the same message. On the graphological level (punctuation, spelling, hyphenation, italicization, paragraphing, line and stanza breaks) the changes are minor. Thus, "the discreet door shut—with a click" and "with a click, the discreet door shut" have very slightly different effects on the reader. The literary magazine I advise sometimes receives revisions of poems accepted for publication, revisions that might seem major to the poets, but are minor to us. When a poem is not working, the case is often that changes in line breaks, wording, or syntax were never the problem to begin with. Rather it seems to be some more basic glitch in the poem's conception—who is speaking to whom and why or, to use Mary Karr's terms, a lack of clarity about the emotion expressed.

It is reasonable to see form and content as variously connected; the more "literary" the form, the less paraphrasable the content. In other words, one could paraphrase (skillfully) a driver's manual without any loss of meaning, but not a novel or a poem. Yet even texts more literary than a driver's manual are paraphrased, separating form from content as they are in Masterplots, Cliff Notes, and Reader's Digest Condensed Books. Furthermore, a translation from one language to another may also separate form and content, but the fact that some translations result in unsatisfying poems points to the importance of form.

Like philosophers and artists, scientists have also entered the debate over surface versus depth, and artifice versus truth. For instance, psychologist Barry Schlenker has discovered that the way people present themselves can actually change how they feel about themselves. Other scientists have shown that acting happy, for example, creates happiness, thus smiling (with the eyes) stimulates the same hormones, whether the smile is spontaneous or deliberate.[16] Thus divisions between inside and outside, surface and depth, and true and false are being questioned and eroded in all fields.

## Standardized Style

Manuscripts and books produced before the seventeenth century exhibit great variance in spelling, punctuation, and capitalization. These were gradually standardized with the help of dictionaries, printing presses, and grammars. Marxist critic and poet Ron Silliman links the trend toward standardized language to capitalism, in which "the illusion of realism and the breakdown of gestural poetic form"[17] make it more possible to have a message that does not call attention to its construction. "Poetry has yielded less (and resisted more) this process of capitalist transformation," writes Silliman, noting, for instance, that poetry is the only genre in which spelling may be unconventional.[18] In the realm of poetry, we might consider "feedback" a kind of standardization, an attempt to make a poem more universally readable; we might consider copyediting another kind. In the publishing industry the number of eyes that looks at a text before it is printed is one indication of its importance and financial viability. Interestingly, poetry is lightly—or not at all—edited, perhaps because of cost or because standardization would destroy the poet's "style."

Judy Grahn's *True to Life Adventure Stories*, published in 1981 by the Crossing Press, resists standardization. Grahn collected working-class women's stories and tried

> to keep each writer's language intact, precise for the story it is telling, for the more closely coordinated we allow content and form of any art to be, the more accurate, useful and whole it is. In addition, when a sentence says, as one of Linda Marie's does, "we could beirly survive on what I could make in any part of the world," I simply don't feel it is appropriate to let Mr. Webster say that what is wrong with the sentence is the spelling.[19]

The line between fact and fiction is blurred in these stories, but Grahn's intent is "truth," suggesting that the barrier to truth is convention. Grahn says the stories she chose are "true": "By true I mean they are based on information which is close to, or is, the original source of the story." They are "lived stories," she says, and the language tells us this is so: "Every word, scene, gesture speaks authentically of the real lives we live as women."[20]

When we turn from stories to poetry with respect to this argument ("the less artifice, the more truth"), we need only consider the dominance of free verse. But it is also important to note that freedom from rules on versification doesn't necessarily mean less artifice. On the one hand, Philip Levine writes, "In my ideal poem, no words are noticed. You look through them into a vision . . . just see the people, the place."[21] On the other hand, l=a=n=g=u=a=g=e poetry—even in the very grapheme of its name—calls attention to form. And in between is a wide range of practice, one that may differ from poem to poem, not just between poets.

Louise Glück, for example, is a poet whose work has remained relatively consistent, and yet in the "Author's Note" to the reprint edition of the first four books of her poems, she distinguishes between books on the basis of syntax:

> After *Firstborn*, I set myself the task of making poems as single sentences, having found myself trapped in fragments. After *The House on Marshland*, I tried to wean myself from conspicuous syntactical quirks and a recurring vocabulary—what begins as vision degenerates into mannerism. And after *Descending Figure*, my favorite of the books here, I tried to learn to use questions and contractions, because I finally noticed that I'd refused them and it seemed interesting to discover how the poems would sound if I didn't.[22]

Glück's distinction between "vision and mannerism" is another way of saying "content and form" or "truth and artifice." The power of Glück's poems comes from psychological insights, which at their best transcend the individual and create myth. Though her simple subject/verb/object sentences may have been elongated slightly over the course of her career, her insights are what make her poems interesting. There is a narrative paraphrasability to them, like that of myth.

# Habitual Syntax

Although American prose has become simpler since the mid-twentieth century, it is still a fact that more practiced writers tend to produce longer and more complex sentences. In addition to the length and complexity of sentences, a writer can learn to study patterns in the use of other elements of syntax: tense, passive versus active voice, sentence types (declarative, questions, imperative), frequency of particular parts of speech, clause type and structure, participial phrases (verb, noun, prepositional), person (first, second, third), and the frequency of fragments. Any one feature in this partial list may become a writer's habit or provide an "opening" for the reader, suggesting possibilities of syntactical analysis.

Habits are revealing, in that they indicate one's response to stress in the past. Moreover, habits may be injurious in the long run. Just as athletes and musicians who perform the same movements in the same way over extended periods of time may actually injure their bodies, certain writing habits may constrict the work of the writer. For instance, many of my undergraduate students were taught by their high school teachers never to say "I" in essays. What no doubt began as a teacher's attempt to professionalize student writing seems to have gone haywire as those students begin to apply the rule without understanding the reason behind it. By the time they reach college, many have developed bizarre ways around this restriction, and my task involves getting them to take responsibility for their ideas, use active voice, and say "I."

Mature and more fluent writers also have their habits. The repeated use of fragments, for example, might reveal an antagonism toward making relationships between things explicit. The usefulness of this habit depends on the rhetorical situation of the writing. Whereas *hypotaxis* (the combination of phrases and clauses with coordinating and subordinating conjunctions such as *if, because, so, since*) is necessary in a critical essay wherein ideas must be linked, hypotaxis might be less important—even contradictory—in a poem or a story wherein a reader is asked to make the "leaps" between images. Conversely, *parataxis* works by juxtaposition, utilizing punctuation such as semicolons and periods as the organizing tools among the ideas. Susan Griffin's nonfiction book about war, *A Chorus of Stones*, repeatedly uses paratactic sequences of short sentences to simulate her comprehension process. In other words, instead of creating sophisticated, complex sentences that suggest she has control over and understanding of the facts, Griffin offers a series of overlapping simple sentences that transmit her own numb bafflement:

> She is across the room from me. I am in a chair facing her. We sit together in the late darkness of a summer night. As she speaks the space between us grows larger. She has entered her past. She is speaking of her childhood. Her father. The war. Did I know her father fought in the Battle of the Bulge? Was it for him, this great and terrible battle? She cannot say. He never spoke of it at home.[23]

Griffin's syntactical practice in this book exemplifies her creativity—a more journalistic venue might very well have demanded a standardized style.

Is parataxis in fact the "dominant mode of our time" and "one of the marks of the postmodern"? The question has been debated by Fredric Jameson and Bob Perelman.[24] Does the very act of linking ideas syntactically assume a mastery and control that belie the state of the world? In other words, does parataxis merely help the writer avoid difficulty? "Sentence length is an appropriate gauge of difficulty because it measures relationships," notes Kevin Catalano. "Longer sentences incorporate more words, and more words mean more relationships which increase the effort for the reader."[25] Perhaps paratactical "sound bites" mirror the flash of unconnected images we see on television and suit our short attention spans.

A poem whose first two sentences use both parataxis and hypotaxis is Stephen Dunn's "Corners":

> I've sought out corner bars, lived in corner houses;
>     like everyone else I've reserved
> corner tables, thinking they'd be sufficient.
>     I've met at corners
> perceived as crossroads, loved to find love
>     leaning against a lamp post

> but have known the abruptness of corners too,
>     the pivot, the silence.[26]

The semicolon that ends the first line creates a sort of corner by linking two independent clauses. The second sentence is hypotactic in its use of "but" to create an opposition between the first part (representing good corners) and the second (representing bad corners). Leaving out the "but" would require the reader to supply the opposition. In this poem, "corners" is a trope for a wide range of things: protection, threat, crossroads, bodies, places, time, and emotions. The syntax controls this range, for example by adhering to a subject/verb/object frame throughout. In other words, the regular syntax helps shape the poem into a syntactical box, with the first sentence (twenty words), second sentence (twenty-eight words), third sentence (thirty-five words), fourth sentence (twenty-three words) and fifth sentence (thirty-five words) broken up into roughly equal bits, like walls to a room. Ancillary to sentence length are clause length and line length, creating a rhythm that corners the reader.

## Syntactical Strategies

The sentence is a grammatical unit, a minimum complete utterance in writing that is fixed by a period. It must have a subject and a predicate, and it can be extended endlessly by appending clauses and phrases. An elegant sentence permits the reader to understand without rereading. It is a train headed to a destination, which the reader knows won't make unscheduled stops. Poems that consist of one sentence must use a range of devices to link ideas, from punctuation to coordination, yet their destinations may remain a surprise until the end. Poets use this stylistic restriction as a spur to creation, much as the poems in Christian Bok's *Eunoia* restrict the use of vowels. Robert Frost's "The Silken Tent" is a one-sentence sonnet, and Carl Phillips has a poem in almost every book with this form, for example, "The Grackle" in *The Rest of Love* and "Trade" in *Rock Harbor*.[27] Consider Lance Larsen's "Spider Luck," which draws attention to syntax by attenuating it:

One toe-nudge too many and she exploded, poor
mother spider, into a slick of babies—no more
than spilled commas, unless you knelt
at the open door with a used paperback of *Beowulf*,

as I did, to rescue them, and happened
to notice the pool playing *hide the button*
with Cassiopeia and wondered about heroic codes
in general and my cowardice in specific

for not swimming naked at 2:30 am and which lunatic
neighbor slipped into my apartment to steal
half a rotisseried chicken while I mailed a letter
and which one I should trust to water my ferns

and why rain is almost never a possessive
and whether I was the only one awake enough
to hear the wind saying with its hundred
mouths, *Never mind, little orphan, never mind.*[28]

It takes skill to write a sentence this long, one that doesn't lose
the thread of meaning as it builds to the end. In "Spider Luck"
the bursting sense of the sentence correlates to the pregnant
mother spider, and also to the speaker's sense of being over-
whelmed by detail and derailed by lost trust. The last two stanzas
follow from the verb "and wondered about": the verb anchors
the speaker's wondering, and puts the last half of the poem
firmly in his mind, not "reality." The end of the poem recalls the
beginning episode of putting the baby spiders outside and the
last consolation is addressed to the spiders and to the speaker.
Breaking the ideas into independent sentences would suggest
that the speaker could control his environment. Confining the
poem to one long sentence signals the speaker as part of his
surroundings.

As Ellen Bryant Voigt points out, poets negotiate the rhythm
of the line against the rhythm of the sentence.[29] Long sentenc-
es can be clarified by short lines. The branching syntax Voigt
notes in poems by Stanley Kunitz and Robert Frost is a common
structure of a certain kind of popular American poem, which
starts with an observation, wanders a bit, and then ends with the

"point." It is also a structure that has been criticized for presuming the hegemony of the speaker and the coherence of the subject. The linguistic category of "end focus" presumes the general tendency for given information to precede new information.[30] In other words, "John wrote the whole book" and "the whole book was written by John" differ in context. The first sentence answers the question, "What did John write?" while the second answers, "Who wrote the book?"

But what if the sentence is not a train with a destination? In poetry, meaning does not convey information as much as instigate the reader's process of discovery. What is considered aberrant in prose might be a virtue in poetry. Everyday speech does not employ devices such as alliteration and inverted syntax, but these are common tools in poetry. For instance, the inverted order of the first lines of *Paradise Lost* signals it as verse: "Of Man's first disobedience, and the fruit / Of that forbidden tree whose mortal taste / Brought death into the world, and all our woe, / With loss of Eden."[31] Starting with the preposition "of" opens a door into the poem, making the first lines an abstract for the rest. "Of" is highly relational, a word that signifies groupings and judgment. The poet Carolyn Kizer once told a Squaw Valley workshop that her favorite trick for starting a poem with energy was starting it with a preposition, in the middle of the action. Another syntactic signal is the use of an uncommon verb form, as in poem #1186 by Emily Dickinson:

> Too few the mornings be,
> Too scant the nights.
> No lodging can be had
> For the delights
> That come to earth to stay,
> But no apartment find
> And ride away.[32]

A more usual way of stating the first two lines would be: "The mornings are too few and the nights too scant." But the poem places verbs at the ends of lines, making us ask, "Too few for what?" and propelling us to the end. Dickinson's choice of "be" signals strangeness and gestures toward the imperative ("be" in another context would be imperative: be well). Although the lines create a complete sentence, they read like fragments because the most important aspect, *why*, is not stated. Moreover, the repetition of "too" heightens the phrasing.

The poem's second sentence buries its subject ("delights") in the middle, which underscores the fleeting presence of those delights. In an essay, this sentence might read as follows: "Because the delights that come to earth do not find lodging, they ride away." Meanwhile Dickinson's use of passive voice underscores the passive quality of the delights, which come to earth like faeries that will not look for lodging explicitly, as if such a search would be too pedestrian for them. The poem exhorts the reader to be on the lookout for delight, and the poem's syntactical oddities not only alert us that we are reading verse, but also make us see what we take for granted. In this case, one might say the strange syntax simulates the ephemeral and estranged quality of delights.

James Joyce's *Finnegans Wake* is a prose work that torques diction and syntax for revolutionary effect. From the first sentence, the novel demands slow reading and a wide range of reference: "riverrun, past Eve and Adam's, from swerve of shore to bend of bay, brings us by a commodius vicus of recirculation back to Howth Castle and Environs."[33] This sentence actually discards the convention of beginning capitalization. Meanwhile "Eve and Adam's" refers to a church in Dublin whose name Joyce reverses. And the teleological irony of the opening is that the first sentence completes the novel's last sentence—a narrative trick that it will take the reader 627 pages to discover. Joyce's lexical wordplay and syntactical oddities shout their difference from classic realism.

How a piece of writing calls attention to form varies on a continuum from exaggeration to error. If one might say that "Spider Luck" exaggerates and *Finnegans Wake* exaggerates more, one might take the argument further and say that the poems of Gertrude Stein err. Much like Louise Glück in realizing her growth through syntax, Stein heralds her discovery of nouns in "Poetry and Grammar" as the gateway to poetry:

But and after I had gone as far as I could in these long sen-
tences and paragraphs that had come to do something else I
then began very short things and in doing very short things
I resolutely realized nouns and decided not to get around
them but to meet them, to handle in short to refuse them by
using them and in that way my real acquaintance with poetry
was begun."[34]

If Stein's prose presents syntactical challenges, her poems offer
more. Here is the first section of "Yet Dish":

Put a sun in Sunday, Sunday.
Eleven please ten hoop. Hoop.
Cousin coarse in coarse in soap.
Cousin coarse in soap sew up. soap.
Cousin coarse in sew up soap.[35]

Is "Sunday" being addressed or just repeated? Why are the num-
bers important? Is "hoop" a reference to embroidery, a game, or
skirts? Do cousins visit on Sunday, as a matter of course, freshly
washed? Why is the fragment "soap" not capitalized while the
fragment "Hoop" is? What is the difference between the last two
lines? The poem resists meaning, resists paraphrase, and makes
me think of Julia Kristeva's revision of the Lacanian realm of the
imaginary. She claims that poetry is one form of language that
can resist patriarchy because it can evade the symbolic realm
and return to the imaginary realm in the course of expressing
itself.

Perhaps readers of poetry are more open to irregularities
than readers of prose. The British poet Donald Davie notes that
"what is common to all modern poetry is the assertion or the as-
sumption (most often the latter) that syntax in poetry is wholly
different from syntax as understood by logicians and grammar-
ians."[36] Examining syntax in poetry through the lens of three
philosopher-critics, T. E. Hulme, Suzanne Langer, and Ernest
Fenollosa, Davie wants to "show the inadequacy of the symbol-
ist and post symbolist tradition" because it articulates only the
world of the poem. In other words, Davie is disturbed by poetry
that abandons reference, such as Stein's, although he names no
names. While he admits that it is poetry, he says he doesn't like

it because it has lost its "humanity": "for poetry to be great it must reek of the human."[37] Davie's sentiment is echoed today by readers who reject poetry without a coherent human speaker, a personality behind or out of the words.

When William Carlos Williams says of e.e. cummings' writing that "it isn't at all english," and goes on to say, "cummings has *come from* english to another province having escaped across a well defended border,"[38] he means that cummings was trying to challenge the ideology of grammar. "With cummings every syllable has a conscience and a specific impact—attack, which, as we know now—is the best defense."[39] It was Gertrude Stein who wrote, "I really do not know that anything has ever been more exciting than diagramming sentences . . . the one thing that has been completely exciting and completely completing. In that way one is completely possessing something and incidentally one's self."[40] It seems Stein believed that ideology works in grammar, and she saw how she could challenge it.

As Marjorie Perloff has shown, Ludwig Wittgenstein's ideas about syntax are similar to Stein's.[41] In *Philosophical Investigations*, Wittgenstein writes,

> When I say that the orders "Bring me sugar" and "Bring me milk" make sense, but not the combination "Milk me sugar," that does not mean that the utterance of this combination of words has no effect. And if its effect is that the other person stares at me and gapes, I don't on that account call it the order to stare and gape, even if *that* was precisely the effect that I wanted to produce.[42]

He asks why it sounds strange to say, "For a second he felt deep grief" and goes on to explain that it is because we understand grief to last longer than a second. In other words, there is a disjunction between sentence meaning and the choice of the word "grief." We know that grief is not a fleeting emotion, so the sentence doesn't make sense. These are the very disjunctions that writers like Stein, Pound, Williams, and cummings explore in their poems. These are the very distinctions that disturb readers like Davie, among others.

Another example of syntactic disjunction can be found in Karen Garthe's poem "Stolen Car," which begins, "Once was a

queen and he didn't deserve cruel treatment."[43] Just as we under-
stand that grief is long lasting, we know that queens are female,
so the use of the male pronoun "he" seems wrong—making us
reread and question what is happening. Is the queen in this case
a transvestite or someone who otherwise has adopted feminine
behavior? Or does the poet merely skip the linking idea, that the
queen was cruel to a male subject? In either case, the syntactical
oddity makes the reader slow down and question not only what
is being said but also what is assumed through the language.

William Carlos Williams said, "Kill the explicit sentence,
don't you think? And expand our meaning—by verbal sequenc-
es. Sentences, but not grammatical sentences: deathfalls set by
schoolmarms. Do you think there is any virtue in that? Better
than sleep? To revive us?"[44] Williams is railing against the ideol-
ogy of grammar, and he praises Stein for "tackling the fracture
of stupidities bound in our thoughtless phrases, in our calcified
grammatical constructions and in the subtle brainlessness of our
meter and favorite prose rhythms—which compel words to fol-
low certain others without precision of thought."[45]

Patrick Moore shows that Williams' own syntax deviated in
ways that advanced his poems: with modifying clauses that cre-
ated separate, floating images, with parataxis, with copulative
verbs, with exclamations and rhetorical questions asserting the
priority of instinct and feeling, with dependent phrases and
clauses before the subject or between the subject and the verb
to temporarily suspend closure and meaning.[46] The question of
when syntactical oddity improves writing as opposed to when it
is the sign of a clumsy or lazy writer is best answered in the con-
text of the writer's oeuvre.

A good end to this discussion of syntax would be to analyze a
poem that exemplifies syntactical fluency. Here is a one by Anne
Carson:

*Shadowboxer*

Of the soldier who put a spear through Christ's side on the
    cross
(and by some accounts broke his legs),
whose name is Longinus,
it is said

that after that he had trouble sleeping
and fell into a hard mood,
drifted out of the army
and came west,
as far as Provencia.
Was a body's carbon not simply carbon.
Jab hook jab.
Slight shift and we catch him
in a moment of expansion and catastrophe,
white arms sporting strangely in a void.
Uppercut jab jab hook jab.
Don't want to bore you,
my troubles jab.
Jab.
Jab.
Punch hook.
Jab. *Was a face not all stille*
*as dew in Aprille*
Hook.
Jab.
Jab.[47]

Even if "Shadowboxer" were printed without line breaks, it would never be mistaken for prose, simply because its syntax demands heightened reading. Reminiscent of *Paradise Lost* and Auden's "The Old Masters," this poem begins with an inversion ("Of the soldier") that creates a somewhat pedantic tone. The initial preposition ("Of") signals family, alliance, and correlation, but the main clause ("it is said") is marvelously empty— marvelous because this emptiness mirrors that of hearsay and history. The title provides the grounding image of the invisible opponent in shadowboxing who is only there for the sake of practice or exercise. It also provides a metaphor: A shadowboxer expends energy for no apparent reason.

In fifty-two words, the first sentence of "Shadowboxing" sets up the story of Longinus, the details contained in the dependent clauses, notably the clause that begins the poem. In this way, Carson front-loads the syntax. She begins the poem with the subjects of betrayal, faith, and violence, rather than leading up to them obliquely, thereby letting readers know where they are. Once she has set up the subject, the syntax shifts to a question, notably one without a question mark, as though the speaker were talking to herself.

Two versions of the Longinus story exist: in one, he converts and becomes a saint after witnessing the miracle of Christ's blood. In Carson's version, the actions of Longinus lead him into despair and he becomes a drifter. Carson also plays with the versions of what happened to Christ's body. In the gospel according to John, an unnamed soldier pierces the side of Jesus as he hangs on the cross:

> Since it was the day of Preparation, in order to prevent the bodies from remaining on the cross on the sabbath (for that sabbath was a high day), the Jews asked Pilate that their legs might be broken, and that they might be taken away. So the soldiers came and broke the legs of the first, and of the other who had been crucified with him; but when they came to Jesus and saw that he was already dead, they did not break his legs. Instead, one of the soldiers pierced his side with a spear, and at once came out blood and water. (John 19:31–34)

The synoptic gospels mention soldiers and the centurion, but not the piercing of Jesus' side with a spear. Furthermore, Longinus is not mentioned by name anywhere in the Bible. Rather we find his story in the apocryphal *Gospel of Nicodemus*: "Then Longinus, a certain soldier, taking a spear, pierced his side, and presently there came forth blood and water."[48] This account, which contradicts John's gospel, has Longinus spearing Christ *before* his death. Carson goes further, linking the story of Longinus to that of the speaker: "don't want to bore you, my troubles jab." This punning sentence signals a speaker who rejects the idea of faith in Christ. The poem also quotes a medieval lyric, "I Sing of a Maiden," an Annunciation piece, wherein Jesus comes as a courtly lover to the bower of his mother Mary:

> He cam also stille
> Ther His moder was,
> As dew in Aprille
> That falleth on the gras.[49]

Carson truncates a refrain in the lyric, making the reference ironic. If Jesus and Mary in the medieval lyric have quiet faces, like dew in April, then Longinus and the pierced Christ have the opposite, *Was a face not all stille as dew in Aprille*. Carson's use of "was a face" instead of "had a face" undoes the opposition between surface and depth: Longinus is reduced to a face, as though his actions represent him entirely, just as the writing of history is a face (surface) that we interpret.

"Shadowboxer's" complexity is linked to its dialogism (or heteroglossia), terms coined by Mikhail Bakhtin to explain how bits of language that come from different systems create friction. Bahktin points out that "this usually parodic stylization of generic, professional, and other strata of language is sometimes interrupted by the direct authorial word."[50] The first sentence of "Shadowboxer" refers to an apocryphal gospel, repeating hearsay, while at the same time formalizing it with inverted syntax and a long sentence. The second sentence is a question that doesn't have a question mark. It could be that this second sentence refers to the Shroud of Turin, which carbon dating has found to be from the 1300s, the same century as "I Sing of a Maiden." Perhaps an ordinary body could not leave a mark, but a holy body could. The next line recalls the boxing of the title—three monosyllables without punctuation describe the moves of a boxer and merge Longinus with the speaker.

"Shadowboxer" contains 113 words, of which 11 are prepositions, 21 are nouns, and 32 are verbs. The abundant verbs underscore the action of the poem and contribute to the sense of present action, as in a fight transcription. And yet the boxing words—*jab, hook*, and *uppercut*—can also be read as nouns (one throws or gives an *uppercut* or *hook*). Moreover, in boxing terms, a jab is a distraction, a setup to a reverse punch or hook, or a method to close the distance from an opponent. A jab is a means to an end, not a way to knock someone out. Carson sets up the reader to become the shadowboxer—as well as the opponent who is jabbed. The reader in Carson's poem feels religion as the "jab hook jab" of a fist in the face. The poem's last word, "jab," underscores the incomplete transmission of history.

According to Ida Rolf, who developed the system of structural integration of the human body that we now call "Rolfing," we don't need to see the whole person to know the structure of the whole body: "Every move he makes tells what his structure is."[51] Rolf's insights about bodywork can be applied to poetic syntax. We might take those insights and apply them specifically to the work, over time, of a writer like Anne Carson. Carson's moves have been irregular, unpredictable except in their very variety. She habitually challenges stasis; even her combination of poetry and prose in her books—*Glass, Irony, and God*, for example— pushes against stasis.

When Yeats said, "As I altered my syntax, I altered my intellect," he meant that change of any kind is not confined to a narrow realm. No change in the human body is without analogue, without consequence elsewhere. Altering the way one moves will also alter the way one thinks. A recent *New York Times* article quotes social psychologist and Harvard Business School professor Amy Cuddy: "'Poses are powerful.' With colleagues, she has, through a series of controlled experiments, shown that assuming an expansive pose (think Wonder Woman with legs planted apart and hands on her hips) for two minutes will increase testosterone and lower cortisol in your bloodstream."[52]

Some take it further, arguing that it does not require a belief in the cosmic relatedness of beings to see that *change* has ramifications beyond the individual self. A quote attributed to Gandhi and used in a variety of contexts, "We must become the change we want to see in the world," means that individuals take responsibility for global change. Changing one's syntax is a place to begin.

*Notes*

1. Gugliemo Cinque, *Adverbs and Functional Heads: A Cross-Linguistic Approach* (New York: Oxford University Press, 1999).

2. Aristotle, *The Rhetoric and the Poetics of Aristotle*, trans. W. Rhys Roberts and Ingram Bywater (New York: Random House, 1954), 164–66.

3. Martha Nussbaum, *Love's Knowledge: Essays on Philosophy and Literature* (New York: Oxford University Press, 1990), 15.

4. Yi-Tu Fuan, *Morality and Imagination: Paradoxes of Progress* (Madison: University of Wisconsin Press, 1989), 64–65.

5. John Locke, *An Essay Concerning Human Understanding*, ed. Alexander Campbell Fraser (New York: Dover Publications, 1959), 146.

6. Mary Wollstonecraft, *A Vindication of the Rights of Woman* (London: Walter Scott, 1891), xxxv.

7. Georg Wilhelm Friedrich Hegel, *The Philosophy of Hegel*, ed. Carl J. Friedrich (New York: Random, 1954), 342.

8. Hegel, *The Philosophy of Hegel*, 394.

9. Dante, *Dante to Cangrande*, trans. James Marchand, Georgetown University, July 16, 2012, http://www9.georgetown.edu/faculty/jod/cangrande.english.html.

10. Fredric Jameson, *Postmodernism, Or the Cultural Logic of Late Capitalism* (Durham, NC: Duke University Press, 1991), 12.

11. Jacques Derrida, *Of Grammatology*, trans. Gayatri Chakravorty Spivak (Baltimore: John Hopkins University Press, 1976), 17.

12. Charles Olson, *Selected Writings of Charles Olson*, ed. Robert Creeley (New York: New Directions, 1966), 27.

13. Mary Karr, *Viper Rum* (New York: New Directions, 1998), 52.

14. Karr, *Viper Rum*, 55.

15. Geoffrey Leech and Michael Short, *Style in Fiction* (New York: Longman, 1981), 127.

16. Barry Schlenker, "The Impact of Self-Presentations on Self-Appraisals and Behavior: The Power of Public Commitment," *Personality and Social Psychology Bulletin* 20, no. 1 (February 1994), 20–33.

17. Ron Silliman, *The New Sentence* (New York: Roof Books, 1987), 12.

18. Silliman, *The New Sentence*, 17.

19. Judy Grahn, ed., *True to Life Adventure Stories*, vol. 2 (Trumansburg: Crossing Press, 1981), 8.

20. Grahn, *Adventure Stories*, 12.

21. Philip Levine, *Don't Ask* (Ann Arbor: University of Michigan Press, 1981), 101.

22. Louise Glück, *The First Four Books of Poems* (New York: Ecco Press, 1995).

23. Susan Griffin, *A Chorus of Stones: The Private Life of War* (New York: Doubleday, 1992), 113.

24. Bob Perelman, "Parataxis and Narrative: The New Sentence in Theory and Practice," *American Literature* 65, no. 2 (June 1993), 313–24.

25. Kevin Catalano, "On the Wire: How Six News Services Are Exceeding Readability Standards," *Journalism Quarterly* 67, no. 1 (1990), 97–103.

26. Stephen Dunn, *Not Dancing* (Pittsburgh: Carnegie Mellon University Press, 1984), 11.

27. Carl Phillips, "The Grackle," in *The Rest of Love* (New York: Farrar,

Straus and Giroux, 2004), 51–52, and Carl Phillips, "Trade," in *Rock Harbor* (New York: Farrar, Straus and Giroux, 2003), 65–66.

28. Lance Larsen, "Spider Luck," in *In All Their Animal Brilliance* (Tampa: University of Tampa Press, 2004). Reprinted with permission of the University of Tampa Press.

29. Ellen Bryant Voigt, "Syntax: Rhythm of Thought, Rhythm of Song," *Kenyon Review* 25, no. 1 (Winter 2003), 144–63.

30. Leech and Short, *Style in Fiction*, 213.

31. John Milton, *Paradise Lost* (Indianapolis: Hackett, 2005), The Online Literature Library, Book 1.

32. Emily Dickinson, *The Poems of Emily Dickinson*, ed. Thomas H. Johnson (Cambridge: Harvard University Press, 1955).

33. James Joyce, *Finnegans Wake* (New York: Viking Press, 1959).

34. Gertrude Stein, *Writings, 1932–1946* (New York: Library of America, 1998), 325.

35. Gertrude Stein, *Writings, 1903–1932* (New York: Library of America, 1998), 363.

36. Donald Davie, *Articulate Energy: An Enquiry into the Syntax of English Poetry* (London: Routledge & Kegan Paul, 1955), 148.

37. Davie, *Articulate Energy*, 165.

38. William Carlos Williams, *Selected Essays* (New York: Random House, 1954), 263.

39. Williams, *Selected Essays*, 267.

40. Stein, *Writings, 1932–1946*, 314.

41. Marjorie Perloff, *Wittgenstein's Ladder: Poetic Language and the Strangeness of the Ordinary* (Chicago: University of Chicago Press, 1996).

42. Ludwig Wittgenstein, *Philosophical Investigations*, 2nd ed., trans. G. E. M. Anscombe (Oxford: Blackwell, 1958), 138.

43. Karen Garthe, "Stolen Car," in *Word for Word: A Journal of New Writing*, October 2004, www.wordforword.info/vol2/garthe.htm.

44. William Carlos Williams, *Paterson* (New York: New Directions, 1946), 189.

45. Williams, *Selected Essays*, 164–65.

46. Patrick Moore, "William Carlos Williams and the Modernist Attack on Logical Syntax," *ELH* 53, no. 4 (Winter 1986), 895–916.

47. Anne Carson, "Shadowboxer," in *Men in the Off Hours* (New York: Knopf, 2000), 27. Used by permission of Alfred A. Knopf, an imprint of Knopf Doubleday Publishing Group, a division of Random House LLC. All rights reserved.

48. *The Lost Books of the Bible* (New York: Bell, 1979), 63–91.

49. Celia and Kenneth Sisam, eds., *The Oxford Book of Medieval English Verse* (London: Oxford University Press, 1970).

50. Mikhail Bakhtin, *The Dialogic Imagination,* ed. Michael Holquist, trans. Caryl Emerson and Michael Holquist (Austin: University of Texas Press, 1981), 301.

51. Ida Rolf, *Ida Rolf Talks about Rolfing and Physical Reality* (Boulder: Rolf Institute, 1978), 193.

52. Kate Murphy, "The Right Stance Can Be Reassuring," *New York Times,* May 3, 2013.

# Rhythm and Repetition in Free Verse, or, the Poet as Witch

In a highly influential set of lectures later published as a book, *How to Do Things with Words,* philosopher J. L. Austin inaugurated what is known as speech act theory.[1] He divides spoken language in two categories: "constative speech acts" that say something, and "performative speech acts" that do something.

Most speech acts are constative. "The meeting will be this afternoon." This constative speech act says something. Less common are the performative speech acts, which include vows, epithets, and promises. Performative speech acts don't merely describe something, but actually accomplish the act to which the sentence refers. For example, when a couple says "I do" during a marriage ceremony, they are performing the marriage. Interestingly, Austin considers poetry, along with jokes, to be *neither* constative nor performative. Because of its rhythmic repetition and emphasis on sound as opposed to meaning, Austin considers poetry to be language that neither says something nor makes something happen.

In his elegy for Yeats, W.H. Auden famously took up the argument of poetry's power:

> For poetry makes nothing happen: it survives
> In the valley of its making where executives
> Would never want to tamper, flows on south
> From ranches of isolation and the busy griefs,
> Raw towns that we believe and die in; it survives,
> A way of happening, a mouth.[2]

In the last line, Auden refines his initial assertion that "poetry makes nothing happen." Poetry is rather "a way of happening, a mouth"—the global process of change.

To understand poems as "a way of happening," to access them more deeply, we pay attention to our experience of them in the body. We pay attention to their rhythms: even while reading a poem silently, one hears the words and feels the rhythm. Changing one's rhythm means changing the way one *feels*, and that is no small feat. Physiologists have shown that "rhythmic vocal recitations enhance cardiovascular activity" as well as enhance the baroreflex response that stabilizes blood pressure.[3] In his essay "Listening and Making," Robert Hass points out that "because rhythm has direct access to the unconscious, because it can hypnotize us, enter our bodies and make us move, it is a power. And power is political. That is why rhythm is always revolutionary ground."[4] When experiencing someone else's poem— someone else's rhythms—readers are in a way "ventriloquizing," an experience both daring and safe.

For obvious reasons, scholars have studied rhythms in poetry more often in poems that are metrical. But the scholars Charles Hartman, Derek Attridge, and G. Burns Cooper have, at length and with precision, treated the subject of rhythm in free verse. Hartman defines poetic rhythm as "the temporal distribution of the elements of language."[5] Attridge defines rhythm as an "engine":

> the continuous motion that pushes the spoken language forward, in more or less regular waves, as the musculature of the speech organs tightens and relaxes, as energy pulsates through the words we speak and hear, as the brain marshals multiple stimuli into ordered patterns. To understand and enjoy poetry means responding to, and participating in, its rhythm—not as one of a number of features that make up the poetic experience, but as the heart of that experience.[6]

"Speech always *happens*," Attridge says, "as a process of unfolding sounds and significations, echoing and anticipating each other." In this way, "poetry aims at a precision that makes every word count as something experienced meaningfully through the body at the same time as it is understood by the mind."[7] Cooper analyzes recordings of poems recited by T. S. Eliot, Robert Lowell, James Wright, and others, arguing that their "rhythmic effects" are distinct and idiosyncratic, and that poems are constructed differently from prose.[8]

Because English is a stressed language—alternating between strong stress and less stress, between build-up and release—without thinking about it, English speakers follow stressed syllables with unstressed ones. Robert Pinsky points out that one definition of free verse is "that it achieves an intense cadence that is neither prose nor iambic."[9] While some contemporary American poets reject the idea of "meter" as antiquated, most, to one degree or another, do use actual metrical patterns alongside rhythm in the making of their poems. In fact, one could argue that resisting patterns altogether is difficult simply because English is naturally stressed.

T. S. Eliot wrote that "the ghost of some simple metre should lurk behind the arras in even the 'freest' verse; to advance menacingly as we doze, and withdraw as we rouse. Or, freedom is only truly freedom when it appears against the background of an artificial limitation."[10] Contemporary poets, inclined toward that true "freedom" in free verse, are recognizing their common ground. Catherine Wagner, for example, says meter is interesting because of its incantatory potential, as are "the possibilities of moving in and out of measure."[11]

As we have seen, some poems seem to make something happen, while others might be termed "a way of happening, a mouth." It is useful to look at poems wherein sound and rhythm play a particularly integral part in meaning and pleasure. With these poems, we are appreciating—feeling—the rhythmic energy as organic. But before we look at representative poems, it is important to understand the concept of "magic" inherent in the rhythm of language. Spells, incantations, religious chants, prayers—and poems, too—rely on rhythm for their effect. We know that Roman *vates* (priests) were expected to produce both songs and divinations as part of their work, and critics have demonstrated the many links between the magic practices and occult beliefs of ancient peoples and the contemporary practice of religion. Stanley Kunitz argues that a poem is "at once the most primitive and most sophisticated use of language." His emphasis is on the primitive as the more significant: "The priest or shaman of the tribe casting his spell over things was close to the roots of the poetic experience."[12] The scholar Stephen Glosecki points to the lineage from shamanism to verse: "Germanic verse kept its primeval associations with sympathetic magic—with the effective power of the rhythmic word."[13]

"Magic" conjures up images of the witch, the sorcerer, and the shaman, and as we proceed we need to recall the importance of etymology, and explore the origins of the words springing to mind. The word *witch* is sex-linked but not sex-specific. In other words, most but not all witches were women.[14] Diane Purkiss demonstrates how the witch has been configured by various groups throughout history. The Romantic poets, for example, transformed the witch "into a muse, the object of a poetic quest fraught with danger and desire."[15] Purkiss believes that new wave feminism simultaneously figures the female witch as a victim *and* as a source of "primitive" power.

Conversely, the words *sorcerer* and *shaman* are male-linked, and have more positive connotations. Musician Layne Redmond points out that while anthropologists and archaeologists have not seriously considered the possibility of female shamans, her own experience of listening to three tribal Siberian women drummers was "an important clue that women played the drums in earlier shamanistic societies."[16] The act of drumming creates repetitive sound that allows the shaman to travel back and forth between heaven, earth, and the underworld. Similarly, anthropologist Ian Lewis has shown that in northeast Africa both shamanism (usually male) and spirit possession (usually female) are political forces underscored by gender ideology. In other words, women possessed by spirits are actually driving out patriarchal oppression.[17] The point is that, even in less dramatic instances, rhythm can "fly below the radar" of logic, subverting institutionalized power.

And then we might consider the very word *charm*, from the Latin *carmen* ("verse"). There are numerous instances of language used as charm, from the realm of the sacred to the realm of the profane. The sacred sentence of a priest elevating the Host at mass, "Hoc est corpus," is actually the source of the expression "hocus pocus." When Humbert Humbert is masturbating with Lolita on his lap, he recites a spell:

> Suspended on the brink of that voluptuous abyss (a nicety of
> physiological equipoise comparable to certain techniques in

the arts), I kept repeating chance words after her—barmen, alarmin', my charmin', my carmen, ahmen, ahahamen—as one talking and laughing in his sleep while my happy hand crept up her sunny leg as far as the shadow of decency allowed.[18]

In many languages, rhythmic expressions are used *to make something happen*, whether it is a blessing, a remedy, a curse, or a fated formula. Consider the word "abracadabra," an ancient invocation, which was first recorded in the second century AD, in a Latin medical poem, *De medicina praecepta*, by the Roman physician Quintus Serenus Sammonicus. There are many theories as to the origin of "abracadabra." Some believe it came into English via French and Latin from a Greek word *abrasadabra*. But we see that Serenus Sammonicus advises a sick person to wear an amulet around his or her neck, a piece of parchment inscribed with a triangular formula which acts like a funnel to drive out the sickness:

A B R A C A D A B R A
A B R A C A D A B R
A B R A C A D A B
A B R A C A D A
A B R A C A D
A B R A C A
A B R A C
A B R A
A B R
A B
A

"Abracadabra" might also be traced to the Aramaic phrase *avra kehdabra*, meaning "I will create as I speak." Or its source could be three Hebrew words, *ab* ("father"), *ben* ("son"), and *ruach acadosch* ("holy spirit"). Or it might have come from the Chaldean *abbada ke dabra*, meaning "perish like the word," or from "Abrasax," the name of the supreme deity in a Gnostic sect in Alexandria.[19] In any case, the word *abracadabra*—a recognized charm word—represents an instance of language designed to *make something happen*. That it is also a highly rhythmic word featuring repeated syllables is part of its *charm*.

In Shakespeare's *Macbeth*, we can examine scenes featuring witches and find highly rhythmic language used as a charm. Most scholars see the witches as "low" characters, designed to appeal to the crowd through comic or scare tactics, but whether the witches (also called the "weird" sisters—from *wyrd*, meaning "fate") are evil can be debated. Diane Purkiss notes that nearly every Shakespeare play features witchery or magic of some kind, and that "the menace and the pleasure of witchcraft as spectacle lies ultimately in its destabilizing inscrutability."[20] In *Macbeth*, the witches open the play with a promise to "meet again" with Macbeth, a scene that ends with the chanted couplet: "Fair is foul, and foul is fair, / Hover through the fog and filthy air." The witches tell Macbeth that he will be king. They (or the ghosts they conjure) warn him against Macduff, the man not of "woman born," and the march of Birnam Wood. They assure him that "all this is so" (4.1.124). Because they never tell Macbeth that he must kill Duncan to gain the throne (he makes that choice on his own), and because they never lie in their warnings, the witches may be seen as a neutral force. They do not elaborate on how or when Macbeth will become king—which might plant the idea of murder in his mind—and so their warnings are so vague as to be useless. But they do tell Macbeth to "be bloody, bold and resolute" (4.1.65), which causes him to act tyrannically. The witches have been read by Robert N. Watson as exemplifying the contradictions of English Renaissance society, wherein the divine right of a ruler and the authority of the church were questioned, but wherein, at the same time, the act of defying these institutions resulted in punishment.[21] *Macbeth* follows this pattern: the witches tell Macbeth that he shall be king, Macbeth decides to hasten his destiny by murdering the ruling king, the witches predict his death, and he dies without glory or honor.

In act 4, the witches employ the power of rhythmic language, putting Macbeth under their spell, which signals his trouble:

> 1 WITCH. Thrice the brinded cat hath mewed.
>
>  2 WITCH. Thrice, and once the hedge-pig whined.
>
>  3 WITCH. Harpier cries:—'tis time! 'tis time!

1 WITCH. Round about the caldron go;
In the poison'd entrails throw.
Toad, that under cold stone,
Days and nights has thirty-one
Sweltered venom sleeping got,
Boil thou first i' th' charmèd pot!
    ALL. Double, double toil and trouble;
Fire burn, and caldron bubble.
    2 WITCH. Fillet of a fenny snake,
In the caldron boil and bake;
Eye of newt, and toe of frog,
Wool of bat, and tongue of dog,
Adder's fork, and blindworm's sting,
Lizard's leg, and howlet's wing,
For a charm of powerful trouble,
Like a hell-broth boil and bubble.
    ALL. Double, double toil and trouble;
Fire burn, and caldron bubble.
    3 WITCH. Scale of dragon, tooth of wolf,
Witches' mummy, maw and gulf
Of the ravined salt-sea shark,
Root of hemlock digged i' th dark,
Liver of blaspheming Jew,
Gall of goat, and slips of yew
Slivered in the moon's eclipse,
Nose of Turk, and Tartar's lips;
Finger of birth-strangled babe
Ditch-delivered by a drab,
Make the gruel thick and slab:
Add thereto a tiger's chaudron,
For th' ingredience of our cauldron.
    ALL. Double, double toil and trouble;
Fire burn, and caldron bubble.
    2 WITCH. Cool it with a baboon's blood,
Then the charm is firm and good. (act 4, scene 1, *Mac-
beth*)[22]

What makes these lines so memorable? Note first that the
rhymed trochaic tetrameter couplets are set apart by their very
rhythms from the iambic pentameter of the rest of the play. Note
also that the lines begin and end with a stressed syllable, and the

trochees create a pattern of great energy, as if the speech hurls itself into the atmosphere. Moreover the exact rhymes of "double" and "trouble" and "bubble" are humorous and childlike as they emphasize the meter. The names and parts of common and exotic animals (shark, wolf, dragon, goat, etc.) and humans animalized (Turk, Jew, Tartar) are also humorous—or would have been to a Renaissance audience. The image of the witches making a stew of these ingredients (these words) is grotesquely funny, akin to a child making mud pies. Together, these factors make the witches' spell irresistible to readers and audiences.

Contemporary witches also assume that a spell of rhythmic language can make something happen, but are careful to say it must be for a positive purpose. For example, Raymond Buckland's *Practical Candle Burning* outlines various repetitions of practice and chant for particular purposes such as "to settle a disturbed condition in the home" or "to gain power over others"[23] and Janet and Stewart Farrar's *Spells and How They Work* offers "deliberate process[es] for achieving desired aim[s]" through a ritual negotiation of the unconscious and conscious, the rational and irrational.[24] It is interesting that the back cover of Buckland's book declares that "this is a book full of rituals and spells; it is also a book of poetry."[25]

In her poem "Witch Songs" in *Ghost Girl*, Amy Gerstler considers feminine power, revenge, and poetry:

Women really are diabolical.
Ask one, she'll admit it.
*They're all witches under the skin.*
Plotting, scheming, their recipes
Need ingredients like graveyard
Dust and possum teeth.
*Those they have molested fear them.*

. . .
Riddle: what's the difference
Between a recipe and a spell? Answer:
They're the same. Both have wicked intent.

. . .
As she chants their names, one by one,
The winter stars appear.[26]

At the end of this poem, *something happens*—winter stars appear. There is no difference between a witch's spell and a recipe (or a poem), says the speaker of this poem, ironically noting that these forms of language have "wicked intent." While Raymond Buckler claims that his spells in *Practical Candle Burning* are not intended to be wicked, the poet here seems to claim that women's power is *seen* as wicked, no matter what its intent, and that women can revenge themselves, despite the perception that they are victims.

Sylvia Plath's poem "Daddy" is another example of a rhythmic spell/poem. In it the speaker exorcises herself of patriarchal oppression by inverting the traditional marriage vow. In fact, Plath repeats both the inverted marriage vow and the traditional marriage vow in the course of the poem: "I do, I do" is an inverted repetition of "You do not do, you do not do." The exact rhymes of *do/shoe/Achoo/you* echo nursery rhyme and doggerel, yet the content of the poem is anything but innocuous. The monosyllables ending the lines create more vehemence than, say, the rhymes of "double" and "trouble." The speaker has tried prayer—"I used to pray to recover you"—and is now resorting to magic. The opening lines "you do not do, you do not do" are language trying to make something happen:

> You do not do, you do not do
> Any more, black shoe
> In which I have lived like a foot
> For thirty years, poor and white,
> Barely daring to breathe or Achoo.[27]

For her dark poem, Plath calls upon the marriage vow, as well as upon magic, nursery rhymes and doggerel, thereby allying the primitive repetition of language to the sophisticated awareness of patriarchal oppression.

It is no accident that Plath employs the rhythms and echoes of childhood rhymes in "Daddy" as a kind of magic deep in the language. We know that children see language as magic. In his 1888 folklore study of children's counting rhymes, Henry Carrington Bolton points out that children's customs and word games have their roots in the ancient process of drawing lots, of letting "fate" choose.[28] Often, the meaning of the words is not as important as their rhythmic sounds. Sometimes the words are actually meaningless. Thus, if the words aren't *saying* something, then perhaps they are *doing* something. "In many primitive languages," Bolton notes, "numerals are formed from descriptive words. . . . The original sense of the descriptive words [is] lost in the process of time."[29] Numbers progress at regular intervals, producing a pattern of repetition. Indeed, as a poet, I have found that the best way to internalize metrical rhythms, to get the pattern down, is to disregard meaning and write nonsense words or phrases that have the desired stresses.

Allied with their efforts to use the primitive and childlike en route to the sublime, early twentieth-century surrealists and dadaists such as F. T. Marinetti, Hugo Ball, and Kurt Schwitters created sound poems or "verse without words."[30] One might argue that Gertrude Stein's poems also depend on the primacy of sound and rhythm over meaning. Like music, these poems cannot be paraphrased; saying them *is* their significance. Although most contemporary poets believe that the pattern of words carries a music of its own, making notes unnecessary or even contradictory or distracting, a few—Lee Ann Brown, Jack Foley, Lola Haskins, Catherine Wagner, and Anne Waldman, for example—sing their poems during performances, and Hank Lazer's book *Days* includes notes with the poems.

## Tangle Talk and Sprung Rhythm

The pleasure of a sound being repeated with variation is a facet of both music and language. When children acquire language, they delight foremost in the sound of it, as in "ga-ga, googa." Children hear some words as pure sound, or they relate what they hear to what they know. In other words, because "I pledge allegiance to the flag" has no meaning for a five-year-old, she might translate it into "I led the pigeons to the flag." "Ladies and gentlemen" becomes "ladles and jellyspoons." In their study of children's language and lore, Iona and Peter Opie call this phenomenon "tangle talk."[31] Children are expressing their own exuberance in "jingles, slogans, nonsense verses, tongue-twisters, macabre rhymes, popular songs, parodies, joke rhymes, and improper verses," say the Opies, and they further argue that these verbal acts announce the absurdity of the adult world, mock danger and death, and savor the curiosity of language.[32]

Poems employing verbal repetition also do the very things that the Opies list. The Welsh poet Dylan Thomas and British poet Gerard Manley Hopkins, for example, are two modern poets whose verse relies more heavily on sound than meaning. Lewis Carroll's "Jabberwocky," originally published in *Through the Looking-Glass and What Alice Found There* in 1872, is a famous example of language that skirts the edge of sense:

> 'Twas brillig, and the slithy toves
>   Did gyre and gimble in the wabe:
> All mimsy were the borogoves,
>   And the mome raths outgrabe.
>
> "Beware the Jabberwock, my son!
>   The jaws that bite, the claws that catch!
> Beware the Jubjub bird, and shun
>   The frumious Bandersnatch!"[33]

A contemporary U.S. poet who uses language in this way is Paisley Rekdal. In "Dear Lacuna, Dear Lard," Rekdal's ambivalent, agnostic speaker addresses God. The title immediately clues us into the blend: a lacuna is a space, the etymology of which is *pool*, but *lacuna* as a word carries an echo of *kahuna*, the Hawaiian word for a shaman. God, of course, is the ultimate "Big Kahuna," a slang term. The second half of the title suggests the expected (*Lord*) with "lard"—fat from animals, but a word often used derogatively in our weight-conscious culture. The poem also owes a debt to the sprung rhythms of Gerard Manley Hopkins, in that it has more stressed syllables than unstressed, which make the poem feel top heavy and dense. While critic Paul Fussell says that comedy and wit are unlikely in sprung rhythms, I think Rekdal proves him wrong. Her poem, full of tangle talk, begins:

> I'M HERE, one FAT cherRY
>   BLOSsom BLOOMing like a CLOD. . . .

> . . . Yet plea-bargaining and lack of conversation
> continue to make me
>
> your faithful indefile. I'm lonely. I've turned
> All rage to rag, all pratfalls fast to fatfalls for you,
>
> Mr. Farmer in the Dwell. So struggle, strife,
> so strew me, to bell with these clucking mediocrities..[34]

Part of the pleasure here is in hearing "your faithful inde-file" instead of *infidel*, "farmer in the dwell" instead of *farmer in the dell*, "strew me" instead of *screw me*, "to bell with" instead of *to hell with*. Hearing both the received and tangled versions of the phrases makes us laugh. It is also an example of conceptual blending, the highly sophisticated kind of thinking that Turner and Fauconnier outline.[35] Nearly every couplet contains a tangle that carries through the poem like a roller coaster. Later in the poem, Rekdal puns on her own name: "Hello, joy. I'm thirsty. I'm Pasty Rectum." "Thirsty" puns with *thirty* and "Pasty Rectum" with the name *Paisley Rekdal*. The merging of high religion and the sanctity of one's name is undermined by a low bodily reference, a child's blasphemy.

Religion gets tangled in another way in Kamau Brathwaite's poem "Sam Lord," about a Barbadian folk hero and pirate. The poem alternates lines of the Lord's Prayer with Brathwaite's own ironic commentary, a commentary that highlights the negative aspects of both Christianity and capitalism.

> The lord is my shepherd
>
> he created my black belly sheep
>
> he maketh me to lie down in green pastures
>
> where the spiders sleep
>
> . . .
>
> my cup of hands runneth over

> surely goodness & mercy. francina & faith
>
> will follow me all the days of my life
>
> & i will dwell in the house of the merchant[36]

Lola Haskins' "The Ballad of Foot-and-Mouth, West York-shire, 2001" accomplishes yet another sort of tangling. Haskins employs counting rhymes (in italics) from the north of England, which date back at least to the early nineteenth century, according to Henry Bolton. The title refers to "foot-and-mouth disease" but also puns on the contrast between sheep calling (mouth) and sheep tracking (foot). The regular rhythm of the poem serves a mnemonic function: it's easier to remember because of the regular patterns:

> *One-ery, Two-ery, Ziccary, Zeven,*
> *Hollow-bone, Crack-a-bone, Ten-or-eleven.*
> *Spin, Spun. It-must-be-done*
>
> So they push them up—the ewes,
> The wethers, the lambs, the tups—
> With their yellow dozers like flowers o
>
> *Eena, Deena, Dina, Dust,*
> *Catt'lla, Jweena, Wina, Wust*
>
> With their yellow dozers like flowers o
> The ewes, half-grown lambs, the tups
> In mountains now with their legs stiff up
>
> *Ein, Tein, Tethra, Methera, Pimp*
> *Awfus, Daufus, Deefus, Dumfus, Dix*
>
> In mountains now with their legs stiff up
> The wethers, the half-grown lambs, the ewes
> And what is motherhood now o.[37]

The poem continues alternating stanzas of the sheep-counting song with the poet's commentary refrain on the process. The sheep rhymes are like a spell; the counting recalls both liturgy and nursery rhyme. Haskins' lines of commentary create a rhythm different from the counting. The variety in the numbers/names—some are Celtic (*tethera, methera, pimp*), some Saxon (*zickery, zeven*), others Germanic (*ein, tein*)—adds to the effect of the poem as a delicious soup. I'll try to unravel how the stresses work in the poem:

ONE-ery // TWO-ery // ZICcary // ZEven,
HOLlow-BONE // CRACK-a-BONE // TEN-or-eLEVen
SPIN // SPUN // It-MUST-be-DONE

Note that dactyls set the poem in motion, starting with force and continuing the energy, with the caesuras strongly marked to facilitate the counting. The counting rhymes boom out, while the poet's commentary provides backdrop and integration. The second stanza can be read as iambs or perhaps as amphibrachs, as many of the caesuras seem to add an unheard extra syllable—after the first two lines, for instance. The first line of the second stanza begins with a stressed word, "so," acting as a bridge from the dactyls of the first stanza to the nonmetrical commentary:

SO they PUSH // them UP—// the EWES,
The WEthers // the LAMBS // the TUPS—//
With their YEL // low DOZers // like FLOWers // O

While neither the counting rhymes nor the refrain is exactly metrical, I think both kinds of stanzas carry a strong enough imprint of pattern to place the poem in the category of *song*. Hearing "The Ballad of Foot-and-Mouth, West Yorkshire, 2001" is akin to the pleasure of hearing two hands playing different parts on the piano.


**Repetition and Variety**

Most art depends on the tension between repetition and variety. In *How Are Verses Made?* Vladimir Mayakovsky writes that the "struggle to organize movement, to organize sounds around oneself, discovering their intrinsic nature, their peculiarities, is one of the most important constants of the work of the poet: laying in rhythmic supplies."[38] In her prose poem "Stereo," Anne Waldman lays in rhythmic supplies by repeating words within the rhythms of prose to hilarious effect. Written in the nineties, the poem is prescient in acknowledging marriage as an institution that can be rewritten as same sex. It describes the benefits of marriage by repeating key words that stress twinning, and the poem's length and the excess of its devices contribute to its devastating humor:

Marriage marriage is like you say everything everything in stereo stereo fall fall on the bed bed at dawn dawn because you work all night. Night is an apartment. Meant to be marriage. Marriage is an apartment & meant people people come in in because when you marry marry chances are there be edibles edibles to eat at tables tables in the house. House will be the apartment which is night night. There there will be a bed bed & an extra bed bed a clean sheet sheet sheet or two two for guests guests one extra towel. Extra towel. How will you be welcomed? There will be drinks drinks galore galore brought by armies of guests guests casks casks of liquors liquors & brandies brandies elixirs sweet & bitter bitter bottle of Merlot Merlot Bustelo coffee. Will you have some when I offer. When you are married married there will be handsome gifts for the kitchen kitchen sometimes two of everything. Everything is brand brand new new. Espresso coffee cups, a Finnish plate, a clock, a doormat, pieces of Art. And books of astonishing Medical Science with pictures. Even richer lexicons. When you are married married there will be more sheets sheets & towels towels arriving arriving & often often a pet pet or two two. You definitely need a telephone & a cell phone when you are married married. Two two two two lines lines lines lines. You need need separate separate electronicmail electronicmail accounts accounts. When you are married married you will have sets sets of things things, of more sheets & towels matching, you will have duplicates of things, you will have just one tablecloth. When you are married married you will be responsible when neighbors greet you. You will smile smile in unison unison or you might say he is fine, she is fine, o she is just down with a cold, o he is consoling a weary traveler just now, arrived from across the Plains. She my husband is due home soon, he my wife is busy at the moment, my husband he is very very busy busy at the moment moment this very moment. Meant good-bye, good-bye. When you are married married sex sex will happen happen without delay delay. You will have a mailbox mailbox & a doorbell doorbell. Bell bell ring ring it rings rings again a double time. You do not have to answer. That's sure for when you are married people people understand understand you do not have to answer answer a doorbell doorbell because sex sex may happen happen without delay delay. You will hear everything twice, through your ears & the ears of the other. Her or him as a case case may be be. He & he & she & she as a case case may be be, When you are married married you can play play with names names & rename yourself if you like. You can add a name, have a double name with a hyphen if you like. You can open joint accounts when you are married. Marriage is no guarantee against depression. A shun is no guarantee against anything. Marriage is no guarantee against resolution. Revolution is a tricky word word. Here, you hear here? Marriage is sweeter than you think. Think.[39]

The poem begins with gifts and acquisitions, moves to sex, and then turns to personality (no guarantee against depression), and finally to the institution itself. A revolution in the institution of marriage is when same-sex partners are legalized, yet as Waldman acknowledges, "revolution is a tricky word" when applied to marriage, which is patriarchal and historically conservative. Waldman's poem questions whether such an institution can be reinvented in egalitarian terms.

Like the echo from a set of misaligned speakers, or like a long knock-knock joke, this poem surprises us with the words it repeats. The poem presents marriage as predominantly bourgeois—about acquiring things together, from an apartment to espresso cups. Exaggerating the "twoness" and bounty (casks casks) of marriage, Waldman celebrates and questions such bounty. Note the dryness of the prosaic "extra towel." Being married is no tax break, yet it can be "sweeter than you think." Living with someone makes sex possible at any time, perhaps an ironic idea in light of the deadening effect marriage can have on a sexual relationship.

One of my favorite parts of the poem is the conversation with the neighbors. By replicating the kind of small talk and excuses we make (due home soon, just down with a cold, etc.) when discussing our partners with others, the poem alludes to the difference between the public and intimate versions of relationship. In fact, the whole poem is the public version writ double—from the acquisition of things, to pets, to renaming, the poem points to the *visible* aspects of marriage. The invisible and intimate relationship between two people cannot be described; *that* relationship is both ineffable and uninstitutionalized. In other words, marriage is precisely about those things that are public, legislated, spoken, tangible. But within such a frame we find something that cannot be described, something "sweeter than you think." The poem winds itself down toward the end, slowing the pace of repetition and signaling closure. By using repetition to comment on an institution of doubling, Waldman turns the device in on itself.

Another poem that uses repetition is Margaret Atwood's "Variation on the Word *Sleep*." Repetition slows the reader down and simultaneously makes her pay attention to the difference between the word orders. It also creates a feeling of sensuousness, much like chewing slowly or taking small bites in order to savor an experience. The relatively short lines in this poem also contribute to its sense of leisure and contemplation:

> I would like to watch you sleeping,
> which may not happen.
> I would like to watch you,
> sleeping. I would like to sleep
> with you, to enter
> your sleep as its smooth dark wave
> slides over my head. . . .
>
> (last stanza)
> I would like to be the air
> that inhabits you for a moment
> only. I would like to be that unnoticed
> & that necessary.[40]

The difference between "I would like to watch you sleeping" and "I would like to watch you, sleeping" is subtle but distinct. In the first version, the addressee and sleep are one entity; in the second, the comma's pause between them accentuates the sensuous enjoyment of the speaker in the act. The first version implies that the watcher would like to watch the sleeper sleeping versus other things that the sleeper might do. In the second version, we realize that the watcher wants to watch the person but in that most intimate act, sleeping. The detachment in the first version is replaced by greater intimacy in the second version. Greater intimacy is created by a pause.

The third variation, "I would like to sleep with you," makes the process more active, as if the speaker is realizing that the step after watching the addressee sleeping is being next to him. The four repetitions of the word *sleep* in the first six lines spill out urgently. Note that the word then disappears from the rest of the poem, although the poem contains thirty lines. It is as if the poem transcends the word *sleep* itself, going beyond the apparent meaning into a deep state of trance. The poem also progresses steadily in intimacy until the last stanza where the speaker wants to "be the air that inhabits you." The wish to be "unnoticed" and "necessary" recalls both the act of watching someone sleep and sleep itself. The ethereal quality of the air parallels the wish of the speaker.

The repetition of the phrase "I would like to" unifies the poem and enacts the wishes it contains: "I would like to give you the silver branch" becomes "I would like to follow you," which becomes "I would like to be the air" and, finally, "I would like to be that unnoticed & necessary." The route escalates from external gift to internal air, increasing the sense of the poem's movement. There is a line break before the word "only," which makes the sentence mean two things: first that the speaker wishes for something transitory and ephemeral, and second that the speaker wishes she alone (only I) will have this place of honor in the body of the beloved.

Another form of repetition is a "call and response," a form used by Susan Stewart in "Wings," a poem that to my mind *creates wings* by treating them as real, much like a child's imaginary friend. The poem also suggests divination, the process of asking an oracle for information about the future. The pauses in this poem make it both stately and light, as though infused with air:

If you could have wings would you want them?

    I don't know.

I mean, if you could use them to fly, would you want them?

    Yes, if I could fly.

But they would be really big.

    How big?

They might brush against your knees as you walked, or be
    bigger than some
        doorways.
And what if you couldn't ever take them off?

    I still would want them.

If you couldn't take them off, even if you were going
    somewhere,
        or going to bed, or eating at a table, or you wanted to
        pick
        someone up, you could never take them off?

    Yes, I would. I would still want them.

Because you could fly?

    Yes, because of the flying.

And if they were heavy, or even if no one else had them, and
    even if
your children and their children didn't have them?

    Yes, I think so.

But you would still have arms and hands and legs, and you
   could still
      speak, but you had wings, too. You would want the
        wings, too?

Yes, I would want the wings, too.[41]

The poem continues with another three sets of questions and
answers. In part the poem's charm lies in the simplicity or na-
ïveté of the speakers—of the nature of the questions themselves
as well as the simple diction, for instance "really big" followed by
"how big?" The poem draws from the whimsical questions that
children ask about "impossible" things. We know it is not pos-
sible to have wings, so the inquiries seem fanciful. Yet they are
uttered with gravity, and with precise attention to detail such as
consideration of whether the wings would get in the way "while
eating at a table." By taking this tone seriously, in other words by
treating something that is impossible (having wings) as possible,
the poem makes magic.

   Another charming aspect of the poem is the repetition of
part of the question in the answer, as in the last lines quoted
above—not merely "yes" but "yes, I would want the wings too."
As in Margaret Atwood's poem, the difference between "you
would want the wings, too" and "I would want the wings, too"
is perceptible only in stress, marked below according to the way
I hear them: SPEAK, but you HAD WINGS, too. YOU would
WANT the WINGS, too? The rising tone of the question, fol-
lowed by the falling tone of the answer, creates an effect of wings
flapping through the air, up and down.

## Rhyme

In essence, rhyme is merely the repetition of words, parts of
words, or phrases. The pleasure comes from recognizing the
repeated segment in a new context. Compared to Latin and
Latinate languages with their plethora of same sound effects,

English is a difficult language to rhyme. In fact, some English words—*orange, radio, elephant*—are said to have no exact rhyme. In the Middle Ages, achieving an exact rhyme was regarded as a coup, although by the time of the Renaissance, rhyme was already being abandoned, as in blank verse. In the nineteenth century exact rhymes were overused (e.g., *light/sight, true/blue, moon/June*), with a resulting reaction against them. Today it is far more common for poets to achieve sly and subtle effects with rhyme rather than to rhyme exactly, especially at the end of lines, which strikes contemporary ears as trite.

Contemporary poets generally believe that too much congruence of sound distracts. For example, poems by Derek Walcott and Jacqueline Osherow, two contemporary metricists, stretch for rhymes. Osherow's poem "Analfabeta" rhymes these words: *consonance/magnificence, intangibles/parables, read/aloud, side/head, know/canto, elasticity/feisty, slice/place, away/Dante, unwieldy/melody.*[42] The lines in the couplets of Walcott's *Tiepolo's Hound* skip a line for the rhyme:

> On my first trip to the Modern I turned a corner,
> rooted before the ridged linen of a Cèzanne.
>
> A still life. I thought how clean his brushes were!
> Across that distance light was my first lesson.
>
> I remember stairs in couplets. The Metropolitan's
> marble authority, I remember being
>
> stunned as I studied the exact expanse
> of a Renaissance feast, the art of seeing.
>
> Then I caught a slash of pink on the inner thigh
> of a white hound entering the cave of a table,
>
> so exact in its lucency at *The Feast of Levi*,
> I felt my heart halt.[43]

Both metrical and nonmetrical poems feature internal rhyme, a legacy perhaps of the alliteration and repetition that were crucial to Old English verse. Here, for example, are the first lines of Yusef Komunyakaa's "Copacetic Mingus" from *Neon Vernacular*:

Heartstring. Blessed wood
& every moment the thing's made of:
ball of fatback
licked by fingers of fire.
Hard love, it's hard love.
Running his hands down
the upright's wide hips,
rocking his moon-eyed mistress
with gold in her teeth.[44]

The poem describes what it's like to hear (and see) Charles Mingus play the bass, and the poem's internal rhyme heightens the music, simulating the sounds of strings being plucked: "Heartstring" rhymes with "thing." The "b" of "blessed" is picked up in "ball of fatback" and the "f" of fatback rolls into "fingers of fire." The assonance of that line is created by a repetition of "i" sounds: "licked," "fingers," "fire." The "l" of "licked" is carried by "love," and the "h" of "hard" is echoed in "his hands" and "hips." The "upright's wide hips" relies on assonance of "i," while the following line, "rocking his moon-eyed mistress," relies on the assonance of "o" and the consonance of "m." The knottiness and density of the repetition intensify the absorption of its rhythm. We might recall the airiness of Susan Stewart's "Wings," and note how Komunyakaa's rhythms in "Copacetic Mingus" give the reader little time to pause and think.

Metrical poems that employ rhyme tend to place the rhyme word at regular intervals, usually at the ends of lines, so the meter can be heard more clearly. Thus it is that nonmetrical poems employing rhyme thwart our expectations. As Paul Fussell points out, "One reason Ogden Nash's poems are funny, indeed, is that they offer studiously self-conscious rhymes in an un-metrical texture where we have been taught not to expect rhyme."[45]

Quite a few contemporary poets challenge the precept that end rhyme and metrics must coincide in serious poems. In *Moy Sand and Gravel*, Paul Muldoon uses exact end rhyme in nonmetrical poems. I was not surprised to learn that Muldoon plays the guitar in a band, because the words in his poems seem to create syncopation. The form of the poem "The Goose" is a Petrarchan sonnet broken down into sections, with the volta coming after the eighth line, and the turn to the subject of cancer. Yet "The Goose" is essentially a narrative poem that tells three linked stories—the golden goose as cancer, and two friends' struggles with the disease—an unusual choice for the sonnet form, which tends to stress the lyrical. The poem has the rhythms of prose, but I also hear the ghost of a limerick, with its narrative frame, and longer beginning and ending lines:

*The Goose*

I

When Hermes gave that bit of a goose to the goose farmer
   (a)
it not only laid an egg (b)
packed with gold but its leg (b)
was a scaled-down version of a knight's in armor, (a)

its beak done in a pinch (c)
of gold so fine it might have been beaten by some master
   gilder (d)
described by Pliny the Elder, (d)
give or take a thousandth of an inch. (c)

II

About as deep, then, as the melanoma (f)
they diagnosed in one old friend, so taking it upon
   themselves to dig (g)
a hole in her as long as the main street in Omagh. (f)

III

As if they hadn't already made enough room—(h)
for whatever it is—when they went after another's ovaries
   and womb. (h)
Yesterday she drove down to Newry to buy a bit of a wig. (g)[46]

There is humor here, too, but unlike the sweeter humor achieved by Ogden Nash it is dark and ironic. Muldoon's poems have a self-conscious comic edge that is typically postmodern. So cancer is something good (cells) like a golden goose, but it seems the good has run amok and is out of control. Cancer is the result of a society that has too much gold—that does too much with what the earth gives it. The variations of cells may be seen as ludicrous, like the tone of this poem.

We can readily *see* the rhyme scheme of "The Goose," but because the poem is so resolutely nonmetrical, we *hear* it only faintly. The eye can't miss that the rhyme scheme in II, for example, is *f g f* (melanoma/dig/Omagh). In fact, that sentence wrenches syntax and sense in order to accommodate the end rhyme. There might have been a more natural syntax: "Doctors diagnosed a melanoma in one old friend, digging a hole as long as the main street in Omagh to find it." Note the hole is "long" rather than deep, something of a surprise, so that in III, when "doctors," is replaced by the pronoun "they," the procedures become more ominous, more mysterious.

Because the rhyme of the last line reaches back four lines for its precedent, the poem ends on a particularly solemn note, as if the ending could not be both neatly rhymed and true. Ending on the phrase "a bit of a wig" makes the poem seem glancing or trivial, an appropriate modesty in the face of writing about a friend's cancer in a traditional sonnet, a form that generally suggests control over the subject matter. Thus the poem ends with the irony of "singing," when the story itself ends with death. Omagh, of course, is the Northern Irish town where citizens died in an IRA bombing that British authorities knew about but did not prevent—a subtle link to the idea that cancer also is handled scandalously. "The Goose" is thus a poem that "makes nothing happen," but is a "way of happening, a mouth." In fact, one might say that "The Goose" is a poem that resists the idea that language can do or change anything. Its grimness is anchored in the futility of rhyme, in the inability of language to delight, in the impossibility of magic. The golden goose is cancerous.

In the last fifty years or so, scientists and philosophers have sought to prove that the human body thinks and feels simultaneously, that reason and emotion are not separate entities.[47] Neurologist Antonio Damasio uses new access to the human brain to show that our ability to reason is linked to emotion, and linguists George Lakoff and Mark Johnson show how language itself emanates from body consciousness. These theorists are concluding what poets have always known: the human body thinks as it feels.[48] Poetic rhythm is the ultimate example of this process. When we read or hear a poem, we feel it in the same way we feel our hearts beating or our nervous systems humming. Insights gained in this way offer wisdom inaccessible in other ways. When we pay attention to our bodies' wisdom, when we acknowledge that there are other ways to communicate than words, the ineffable is available to us.

*Notes*

1. J. L. Austin, *How to Do Things with Words* (Oxford: Oxford University Press, 1965).

2. W.H. Auden, *Selected Poems* (New York: Vintage, 1990), 80–83.

3. Nicole Garbarini, "Heartbeat Poetry," *Scientific American* 291, no. 4 (October 2004). 30–33.

4. Robert Hass, "Listening and Making," in *Twentieth Century Pleasures* (New York: Norton, 1985), 108.

5. Charles O. Hartman, *Free Verse: An Essay on Prosody* (Princeton: Princeton University Press, 1980), 14.

6. Derek Attridge, *Poetic Rhythm: An Introduction* (Cambridge: Cambridge University Press, 1995), 3.

7. Attridge, *Poetic Rhythm*, 1. See also Attridge's *The Rhythms of English Poetry* (New York: Longman, 1982), and his article "Rhythm in English Poetry," *New Literary History* 21, no. 4 (Autumn 1990), 1015–37.

8. G. Burns Cooper, *Mysterious Music: Rhythm and Free Verse* (Stanford: Stanford University Press, 1998).

9. Robert Pinsky, *The Sounds of Poetry: A Brief Guide* (New York: Farrar, Straus and Giroux, 1998), 109.

10. T. S. Eliot, *Selected Prose of T. S. Eliot* (Boston: Houghton Mifflin Harcourt, 1975), 34–35.

11. Catherine Wagner, "The Politics of Meter: On Traditional Forms," *Poets.org*, August 31, 2012, http://www.poets.org/viewmedia.php/prmMID/5906.

12. Stanley Kunitz, *Next-to-Last Things: New Poems and Essays* (Boston: Atlantic Monthly Press, 1985), 50.

13. Stephen O. Glosecki, *Shamanism and Old English Poetry* (New York: Taylor and Francis, 1989), 89.

14. See Susanna Burghartz, "The Equation of Women and Witches: A Case Study of Witchcraft Trials in Lucerne and Lausanne in the Fifteenth and Sixteenth Centuries," in *Witchcraft, Women, and Society*, ed. Brian P. Levack (New York: Garland, 1992). See also Lara Apps and Andrew Gow, *Male Witches in Early Modern Europe* (Manchester: Manchester University Press, 2003), and Robin Briggs, *Witches and Neighbors* (New York: HarperCollins, 1996).

15. Diane Purkiss, *The Witch in History: Early Modern and Twentieth Century Representations* (London: Routledge, 1996), 35.

16. Layne Redmond, *When the Women Were Drummers: A Spiritual History of Rhythm* (New York: Three Rivers Press, 1997), 42.

17. Ian M. Lewis, *Ecstatic Religion: An Anthropological Study of Spirit Possession and Shamanism* (New York: Routledge, 2003).

18. Vladimir Nabokov, *Lolita* (New York: Random House Digital, 1989), 60.

19. Michael Quinion, "Abracadabra," *World Wide Words*, March 10, 2006, http://www.worldwidewords.org/qa/qa-abr1.htm.

20. Purkiss, *The Witch in History*, 207.

21. Robert N. Watson, *Shakespeare and the Hazards of Ambition* (Cambridge: Harvard University Press, 1984).

22. William Shakespeare, *Macbeth*, ed. Barbara A Mowat and Paul Werstine, Folger Shakespeare Library Series (New York: Washington Square Press, 1992).

23. Raymond Buckland, *Practical Candle Burning: Spells and Rituals for Every Purpose* (Saint Paul, MN: Llewellyn, 1972).

24. Janet Farrar and Stewart Farrar, *Spells and How They Work* (Custer, WA: Phoenix Publishing, 1990).

25. Buckland, *Practical Candle Burning*, back cover.

26. Amy Gerstler, *Ghost Girl* (New York: Penguin, 2004), 11–13.

27. Sylvia Plath, *Collected Poems* (New York: Harper, 1981), 183.

28. Henry Carrington Bolton, *The Counting-out Rhymes of Children: Their Antiquity, Origin, and Wide Distribution, a Study in Folk-Lore* (1888) (Detroit: Singing Tree Press, 1969).

29. Bolton, *Counting-out Rhymes of Children*, 47.

30. Daniel Albright, *Untwisting the Serpent: Modernism in Music, Literature and Other Arts* (Chicago: University Chicago Press, 1999), 288.

31. Iona Opie and Peter Opie, *The Lore and Language of Schoolchildren* (Oxford: Oxford University Press, 1959).

32. Opie and Opie, *Lore and Language*, 18.

33. Lewis Carroll, *Alice's Adventures in Wonderland* and *Through the Looking Glass* (New York: Signet, 2000), 137.

34. Paisley Rekdal, *The Invention of the Kaleidoscope* (Pittsburgh: University of Pittsburgh Press, 2007), 63–64.

35. Gilles Fauconnier and Mark Turner, *The Way We Think: Conceptual Blending and the Mind's Hidden Complexities* (New York: Basic Books, 2002).

36. Kamau Brathwaite, *Ancestors* (New York: New Directions, 2001), 20.

37. Lola Haskins, "The Ballad of Foot-and-Mouth, West Yorkshire, 2001," *Atlantic Monthly*, October 2002, 72, http://www.theatlantic.com/unbound/poetry/antholog/haskins/ballad.htm.

38. Jon Cook, ed., *Poetry in Theory: An Anthology, 1900–2000* (Oxford: Blackwell, 2005), 147.

39. Anne Waldman, "Stereo," in *Marriage: A Sentence* (New York: Penguin, 2000), 25. Used by permission of Penguin, a division of Penguin Group (USA) LLC.

40. Margaret Atwood, *Selected Poems*, vol. 2, *1976–1986* (New York: Mariner, 1987), 77.

41. Susan Stewart, *Columbarium* (Chicago: University of Chicago Press, 2003), 100–101.

42. Jacqueline Osherow, *Dead Men's Praise* (New York: Grove Press, 1999), 26.

43. Derek Walcott, *Tiepolo's Hound* (New York: Farrar, Straus and Giroux, 2000), 7.

44. Yusef Komunyakaa, *Neon Vernacular: New and Selected Poems* (Middletown, CT: Wesleyan University Press, 1993),72.

45. Paul Fussell, *Poetic Meter and Poetic Form*, rev. ed. (New York: McGraw-Hill, 1976), 77.

46. "The Goose" from Paul Muldoon, *Moy Sand and Gravel* (New York: Farrar, Straus and Giroux, 2002), 76–77. Copyright 2002 by Paul Muldoon. Reprinted by permission of Farrar, Straus, and Giroux,LLC.

47. Antonio Damasio, *Descartes' Error: Emotion, Reason, and The Human Brain* (New York: Penguin, 2005).

48. George Lakoff and Mark Johnson, *Philosophy in the Flesh: The Embodied Mind and Its Challenge to Western Thought* (New York: HarperCollins, 1999).

# Gertrude Stein's Granddaughters

*A Reading of Surprise*

It's said that Elizabeth Bishop's pet toucan was named SAM, as an acronym for the three qualities in poems she prized most: spontaneity, accuracy, mystery. Of course, what readers perceive as spontaneity may be the product of deliberate and intense labor on the part of the writer; ultimately it does not matter how conscious the poet was at the moment of writing. So the first quality, spontaneity, is something I prefer to call "surprise," because that puts the emphasis on the reader, and it is the process of *reading* poems that is my focus here.

Modernist and postmodernist poetry is usually considered more surprising than its predecessors, a shift attributed to such factors as psychoanalysis, world wars, atomic power, computers, and globalization. In fact, contemporary readers expect to be surprised, and in some cases they consider surprise to be *the* criterion for good poetry. Robert Bly's term "leaping poetry," which he coined in the seventies, is a case in point: "In many ancient works of art we notice a long floating leap from the conscious to the unconscious and back again, a leap from the known part of the mind to the unknown part and back to the known."[1]

But distinctions between conscious and unconscious minds are difficult for the reader of a poem to determine. Moreover, distinctions between other binary oppositions, such as those between emotion and reason, and between mind and body, are increasingly being questioned by philosophers, as well as by neurologists like Antonio Damasio.[2] To the reader it doesn't matter *how* surprise happens, as long as it does happen. In fact, reader-response theory argues that a text *exists* in the mind of a reader: he or she must "fill in the blanks" or "make the leaps" between ideas in a poem. Thus the act of reading is as creative as the act of writing.

A writer considered by many scholars to be a postmodern writer—and thus surprising—is Gertrude Stein. Stein recognized—and put into practice—the sometimes arbitrary nature of signs, syntax as ideology, and the dependence of language on context. Her work is full of associative leaps, as well as puns, wordplay, and shifts in tone, diction, and syntax. Her emphasis on pronouns (as compared to the imagists' and futurists' emphasis on nouns) indicates her awareness of the referentiality of language and her critique of the self-sufficient image. As Marjorie Perloff points out, Stein "took the naming function of language to be its least challenging aspect."[3]

Though Stein's fabulous syntactical gymnastics have served as an inspiration to many poets, my focus here is on her surprising and playful tone. Stein can be serious without being pompous or pretentious, and her writing has a good-natured quality that never condescends to the reader. It manages to remain deeply funny while at the same time it critiques and theorizes. Her light touch is often best heard in the poems when read aloud. Consider these lines from her posthumously published love poem "Lifting Belly": "You see what I wish. / I wish a seat and Caesar."[4] I hear the echo of *seize her* and I laugh. Stein's poems never let us forget the link between the verbal and physical, the fact that the body produces sound and that both body and sound change constantly.

Before we move from Gertrude Stein to other poets, it helps to think further about the element of surprise itself, and its power over us. When I study a poem, I see it as an engine firing, and only *those* words, in *that* order, can make it fire. But this happens only in retrospect, because at the moment of reading, something else can take place: surprise. Often in the poems I love, the poet thwarts my expectations: by using a word I would not expect, a strange syntactical construct, an omission, an unexpected tone, diction, or some other shift. Such moments have been studied—and prized—by a variety of thinkers since the nineteenth century, including the philosopher Immanuel Kant,[5] the formalist Roman Jakobson,[6] the psychoanalyst Jacques Lacan, and, most recently, the poet and literary theorist Susan Stewart.[7] Surprise is part of what Octavio Paz calls the "principle of variety within unity":

> Repetition is a cardinal principle in poetry. Meter and its accents, rhyme, the epithets in Homer and other poets, phrases and incidents that recur like musical motifs and serve as signs to emphasize continuity. At the other extreme are breaks, changes, inventions—in a word, the unexpected. What we call development is merely the alliance between repetition and surprise, recurrence and invention, continuity and interruption.[8]

Moments of surprise are moments I initially question, trying to decide whether the poet has earned the right to make that kind of leap. When I'm reading, my first reaction is disbelief, followed by some testing: *Can this be true? Do I "buy" the shift?* But in the end, if the poet has done her job, there's the pleasure of having something I take for granted shaken up. And thus I am *changed*—but safely so, because while I feel it in my body, I am actually seeing it on the page, cushioned by paper, by the distance art provides. A surprise, unlike a shock, is pleasurable. The difference, I would say, is the reader's safety and level of preparation for the shift.

And this shift is often accompanied by humor. As philosopher John Morreall points out, "Laughter results from a pleasant psychological shift."[9] Surprise is a primary emotion, on a par with joy, sadness, fear, and anger. It is, as one psychologist describes it, "a highly transient reaction to a sudden and unexpected event . . . one of the most easily and universally recognized emotions."[10] In a poem, this moment of halting is the moment when the brain is trying to make sense of the shift; it is, I think, the essence of the power that a surprise has over us.

Psychologists also consider surprise to have integrative power because it "indicates the need for a shift within the hierarchy of control." Thus, surprise is valuable because it promotes the sort of mind-clearing that is rare in everyday life but ultimately moves our civilization forward. Sylvan Tompkins describes surprise as a "resetting" state because, for a fraction of a second, the mind is cleared of thought.[11] This "resetting" or these "shifts of hierarchies of control" are what enable us to go from one way of thinking—that of the dominant ideology—to another, freer way of thinking.

Once again etymology sheds light on our topic of discussion. The word "surprise" comes from the Latin *sur* ("over") and *prise* ("to take"). When one is surprised, one is taken over—and that's the key to the pleasure. As at the moment of orgasm, one feels not so much out of control as blissfully *taken over* by something greater than we are. (Psychologists have noted that the physiological correlates of surprise are those of "increased arousal.") Surprise also helps us learn: psychologist Leon Kamin points out that "a stimulus must be surprising to produce conditioning"[12] and psychologist Wulf-Uwe Meyer reveals that surprise increases memory.[13] Thus, tiny moments in poems have broad social implications: because of the changes it enacts in its readers, poetry is a way to change the world. The tiny "resettings" that take place when we read a poem prepare us for other, larger "resettings."

The ideological implications of surprise are apparent in theorist Amittai Avivram's definition of surprise as "marked choices against default assumptions."[14] It is these default assumptions that represent ideology—what we perceive to be "normal" in a world where choice is illusory. For example, one default assumption is that speakers in poems are white. Unless we have cues that tell us otherwise (for instance dialect, name, or setting), we assume speakers to be white because in the United States of America the white race is dominant. Default assumptions often privilege one set of binary oppositions over another: white, male, light, straight, reason, mind, and so on. Default assumptions are the stuff of greeting cards and conventional wisdom: *mothers love their children, old people are wise, God is good*, etc. I am not saying that these default assumptions are never true, only that sometimes they are not. Poetry surprises us by challenging these assumptions in an intimate and immediate context.

Which brings us back to Gertrude Stein. In what follows I shall look at poems by five American women—Jeanne Marie Beaumont, Amy Gerstler, Mary Ruefle, Brenda Shaughnessy, and Belle Waring—poets I think of as granddaughters of Gertrude Stein, for they share, in very different ways, her sense of poetic fun and surprise. This is not to suggest Stein has no grandsons, or that surprise is the province of women. But Stein's originality stems in part from the fact that she was writing against the patriarchal tradition of poetry. As she says in "Patriarchal Poetry," "Let her be let her. / Let her be let her let her try. . . . Never to be what he said. . . . Not to let her to be what he said not to let her to be what he said."[15] Perhaps it is not a coincidence that these contemporary women poets are, as Stein was, outside the center of literary power that is mostly white, male, Christian, academic—a center of power that takes itself very seriously. It's possible that funny, quirky, and surprising poems can enact deep changes in the way we think. As Stein says, "For a long time everybody refuses and then almost without a pause everybody accepts."[16]

These poems represent the poets at various stages in their careers. They are poets whose work I want to herald because I reread it with such delight. I find their poems charming, in the original sense of that word—*magical.* Their poems create magic with the seeming effortlessness of Gertrude Stein. I am not suggesting Stein as an "influence" on these poets, because influence is sometimes difficult to trace, and an often fruitless topic of discussion. For instance, how does one trace influence through the generations, knowing, for example, that Wallace Stevens read Stein, and that most contemporary poets read Stevens? In any case, Stein's poems are part of our common language, and it doesn't matter whether these poets read her or not. My method is to point out moments of surprise in their work and attempt to categorize these moments, with the understanding that their poems contain much more than I can discuss here. We begin with Jeanne Marie Beaumont's "The Valley of My Attention." Keeping in mind that the kinds of surprise at a poet's disposal are analogous to poetry's whole bag of tricks (word choice, syntax, white space—devices that are employed in the service of shifts between language, time, or belief systems), we might look at this poem with respect to one element only, *the sound* of the words. That particular element actually bridges the larger categories of surprising shifts. The poem begins with these three lines:

> Fertile and otherwise
> terrain of rest and discovery.
> Place between your outstretched legs. [17]

If you are like me, when you read the word "valley" in the title followed by the word "fertile," you imagine a geography of mountains and valleys: say, the delta of the Mississippi. "Rest" and "discovery" call forth the image of explorers. The white space of the poem also suggests a river carving out a valley from the elevations at its sides. So when I get to the phrase "your outstretched legs," I'm surprised. I go back and, of course, the analogy between body and geography is clearly in place from the very title. The poet planted both pillars of her structure, but it took me until the third line to see them both.

But the *sound* of the word "legs" is also an important ingredient in the surprise. The other words are the Latinate words of geography: "fertile," "terrain," "discovery," even "outstretched." Then comes the heavy thud of "legs," the humble monosyllabic body part. In these three lines alone, the simultaneity of the body and geographic terms is like the simultaneity of the narrated event and the speech event—the relationship between the story and its sounds/absence of sound in white space. As a reader, taking in the clues that help me to "get it," I already feel that I'm in the hands of someone who knows what she is doing. In other words, upon analysis, good surprises in good poems are part of the grand design: The way it looks, how it sounds, and what it means are all working together.

It goes without saying that different readers have different tolerance levels for certainty and surprise, and some might argue that every line should jolt the reader. But most poets play with one element of the language or poem at a time. Sometimes they choose which element to play with in a particular poem. Or they gravitate toward a certain field of play because of who they are. The more elements poets play with simultaneously, the more readers are lost, because many people don't want to play that hard when they read.

For readers, the first step toward this flexibility of thought is resistance against assumptions. We do this instinctively, for example, when we avoid identifying roses as sweet-smelling or the sky as blue. But it takes a certain quantity of "known" to act as ballast for the "unknown." Mary Ruefle's "The Cart" provides just that sort of ballast. The poem surprises the reader with rapid contextual shifts in each and every line, and yet at the same time it contains itself, ending in the neighborhood where it began:

> The empty grocery cart is beginning to roll
> across the empty parking lot. It's beginning to act
> like Marlon Brando might if no one were watching.
> It's a joyous sight, but it might not end all that
> happily, the way someone light in the head
> does something charming and winds up dead.
> My thoughts are so heavy, you couldn't lift
> the bier. They are so light and stray so far
> someone in a uniform wants to bring them in.
> The world might be in agony, but I don't think so.
> Somewhere a woman is swathed in black veils
> and smiling too. It might be the eve of her baptism,
> the day after her son hit a pole.
> How can she signal her acceptance of life?
> What if a hummingbird enters her mouth? I hate
> the thought, whizzing by in red clothes.
> Yet I admire its gloves. Hands are unbearably beautiful.
> They hold on to things. They let things go.[18]

We follow the speaker the way the eyes follow the rolling grocery cart, and at the end, the poem comes back to the idea of hands letting the cart go. If the poem didn't come back to hands and letting go, it wouldn't be as satisfying—the "mind journey" might seem aimless. Yet the poem is not narrative; that is, it's not the story of a rolling grocery cart or the person who sees it.

"The Cart" is a series of reversals. In that way, it exists between certainties, in the space that is truly the space of poetry. It perches between the binary oppositions it presents: heavy/light, dead/alive, happy/unhappy, empty/full, holding on / letting go, being covered / being exposed. And it reverses the usual hierarchy of these concepts. Being alive is better than being dead, as is being happy, full, covered, and holding on. For example, "Somewhere a woman is swathed in black veils / and smiling too." Like the moment of the cart's rolling, the poem is in motion; its betweenness is its message. Note we are not told the full story of the cart, for it seems it is not important whether or not the cart hit something, only that it *might*. I'm reminded of Jacques Delteil, the French surrealist, who wrote, "I believe in the virtue of birds, and a feather is all it takes to make me die laughing."[19] Similarly, Ruefle's poem hinges on its deeply surprising contradictions.

Ruefle's work is riddled with surprise, yet her surrealist sensibility is meshed with tough intellect. Upon close examination, her poems "hold up" to scrutiny; the leaps make a kind of (non) sense and do not seem random. In another poem, "Tilapia," she also shifts contexts, this time meshing "restaurant" and "biblical" references to surprise the reader.

> I walk into the restaurant, a genetic legacy.
> I feel like eating a little fish fried to death
> with a sprig of parsley over one eye.
> You have to engage your dinner in its own mortality!
> At the same time you must order what you want.
> This fish (Til AH pee ah), from humble origins along
> the Nile, is popular in Israel but did not vault to stardom
> until raised in earnest by Costa Ricans.
> From exposure you will gain success or die.
> Christ did both and this is the fish (my waiter's word)
> that He multiplied and thrust upon the multitudes.
> A miracle that it should lie before me! A miracle
> that if I remove the silver backing—courage!—
> I am invited to partake of its tender core. And thus
> tenderly do I love thee, little fish, even as I suffer
> the death of my mother and the death of my father
> and the death of all our days. I will rinse my mouth.
> I will rise from this table and read meaning into the sea.
> I will depart through that revolving door, which knows
> no beginning and no end, and upon my re-entry
> into the burning thoroughfare, I will thread my way
> through the crowds, I will come upon a humble fruit stand,
>     where
> in your name and the name of thousands just like you, I will
>     ask
> for a lemon. This act, ounce for ounce, if executed
> in perfect faith, will rip the cellophane off the world.[20]

The most surprising moment in the poem for me is this line: "Christ did both and this is the fish." When I look back, I see that

I am prepared for that leap with the mentions of mortality and Israel and origins, but nevertheless this line opens the poem in a new and deeply satisfying way. The rest of the poem, with its meshing of "biblical" and "restaurant" language, builds to a close with the speaker asking for a lemon, an act that both completes the eating of the fish and will, "if executed in perfect faith," rip the cellophane off the world. What cellophane? The cellophane that prevents direct experience, that prevents change. Just as the citric acid of the lemon can dissolve cellophane, the poem exposes a level of thinking about faith that is not "the deeper layer" (as though the restaurant and fish discussion were mere window-dressing), but rather something dependent on it. The silver backing is the reason for the tender core and the restaurant meal is the reason for the faith discourse. This strategy is different from the one where the poet uses a "trivial" experience at the beginning of a poem in order to expound on a matter of greater importance later on. Conversely, Ruefle's poem is made of the material it speaks about; the medium *is* the message, as both Gertrude Stein and Marshall McLuhan would agree.

Another kind of surprise is a shift in address, or rather, a shift in the reader's perception of who is being addressed. Belle Waring's poem "Look," the first poem in her book *Dark Blonde*, begins

Your street at sundown.
Your window, the only one lit up

in all those apartments
stacked silhouette black

against the sky—what a color!
like Sargasso—

loud, like they threw blue dye in it.
Citizen, look up,

the sky god is speaking.
Man, that blue is talking.[21]

The second-person address of the poem initially reminds me of Alan Jay Lerner's song "On The Street Where You Live," from *My Fair Lady*. From the first two stanzas, I'm primed to take this as a love poem (the specificity of the apartment description, for example), so that when I get to the word "Citizen," I feel a rush of surprise—Hey, she's talking to me, not some personal loved one. I'm not an eavesdropper, I'm the reason for the poem! The genius of this move has to do with the conflation of the particular with the universal. In the initial reading, the speaker is looking at one lit window from the outside. The surprise is in realizing that I, the addressee, really am inside that window, and that I am being asked to look outside at the blue sky.

A kind of surprise in poetry that is harder to discuss is the element of tone, because shifts in tone are often subtle and nuanced. Tone is the writer's attitude toward the subject or audience or both. Sometimes in discussing tone it is helpful to pin a provisional adjective to the word "tone." We speak of a "serious" tone, or we say it is "ironic," or "sly." But such adjectives are invariably crude compared to the complexity of a poem's actual enactment of tone. Sometimes the tone shift is encapsulated in a single word, as in one line of Belle Waring's poem "Use the Following Construction in a Sentence": "my hot new herringbone date pipes up / *you're such a sensitive girl.*"[22] The key to surprise in this phrase is the word "herringbone," which refers to a pattern of wool used in suits, a pattern that takes its name from the skeletal shape of a herring, a fish. With this word the tone shifts from serious to sarcastic, and I realize that the speaker is making fun of her date. Notice also the way "herringbone" sticks out in the line, the only polysyllabic word in a row of monosyllables. That adds punch. Waring adds irony to the situation of the date by using the words "hot" and "new" with the herringbone image—a man in a herringbone suit is anything but "hot." (Imagine, instead, the date wearing leather.) I also love the way "pipes" is a verb in this phrase. That is, a man wearing a herringbone suit might also smoke a pipe. No surprise. The surprise here, however, is that Waring uses "pipes" as a verb—a verb usually used with children's speech. For example, children pipe up, with little noises interrupting the conversation of adults. In one stroke, Waring has taken the wind out of this date's sails, reduced him to an interrupting child. The irony is further under-scored by what the man says: He calls the speaker a "girl," when at this point in the sentence we already see him as a slightly ri-diculous figure, acting older than he is with a herringbone suit and a patronizing figure of speech.

Jeanne Marie Beaumont's poem "Excavation" employs tone shifts for another kind of critique. The poem seems to me to be a commentary on American capitalism, one that exposes lan-guage as ideological:

> What the water said      if the shoe fit
>         whether the boat ever drifted to shore
>                 did the meek inherit      where the doorway led
>         when the end began      what only hairdressers
>         knew for sure what burned in the fire
>             who started it      how often it rained
>                 which grains were grown to ferment
>                     who bent to pick up the flowers
>                 what scent was left      flag remnants jars
>         what dreaming meant      length of teeth
>             where the buck stopped      ways to spell relief
>                 who said it first      who was buried in June
>         what shapes spoons were      the median rent
>             what the wish was of who blew out the candles
>                 who dimmed the lights      how long nights
>                     were
>         customs of tailors      how they carried their young
>             outdoor marketplaces      misguided beliefs
>         stars' names    coin shapes   which pets   which pox
>             who turned the woman's head      painted it turned
>                 whether the neck was broken      what parts
>         were accident      free prizes from every box
>             what color      the day was[23]

There is a surprising mix of public and private languages in this poem. The reader discovers pieces of platitudes and ad-vertising slogans alongside the biblical phrase, "did the meek inherit." The poem presents us with the bits of language that might remain after disease, accident, fire, dream. Note that the three advertising slogans, "ways to spell relief" (Rolaids), "what only hairdressers knew for sure" (Clairol), and "free prizes from every box" (Cracker Jack), are not presented with the actual names of their products, a move that accentuates the dislocation and relies on the reader to supply the source. Beaumont braids together platitudes like "if the shoe fit," and "where the buck stopped" with stranger phrases like "length of teeth" or "what the water said." Thus, the juxtaposition of these bits of language against other bits of language creates surprise if for no other reason than that we don't expect to see them together. Beaumont is an anthropologist excavating the debris of our language; like pieces of pottery, these phrases represent our culture. And the reader accompanies her on her "dig." Indeed the reader creates the very dig by supplying context and story.

The Russian formalist Mikhail Bakhtin argues that all language consists of bits and pieces taken from diverse contexts—he called this dialogism (or heteroglossia)—and that this inconsistency is not something to be ironed out but rather something to be celebrated.[24] He applied his theory of dialogism only to the novel, but I think that poems like Beaumont's "Excavation" are proof that all language is dialogic. In fact, because the space of the poem is more compressed than that of prose fiction, the effect of dialogism can be more remarkable. In "Excavation," dialogism *is* the poem. Dialogism is valuable because it points to the differences in language systems; their juxtaposition produces mind-altering surprise.

In contrast to Beaumont's formal inventiveness and use of white space, Amy Gerstler's poems are formally conventional: they adhere to the left margin and use stanza breaks and line lengths conservatively. Yet in this sea of certainty are many strange fish: Gerstler's surprises often result from the contrast between her tone and her subjects. Look at the end of "Request," a love poem in which the speaker imagines the object of desire suddenly coming to his or her senses, a hundred years hence:

I hope, at that moment
of gradual, future warming,
that your resistance
to my well-intentioned advances
has thinned to an obstacle
I can bite through

with a delicate snap,
like a rice cracker.
I pray you'll no longer
refuse my adoring overtures
as we pass through bamboo forests
populated by monkeys
who shower us with bruised fruit
and human babies they've kidnapped,
who tumble into our arms, unharmed.[25]

The surprising pleasure here is the contrast between the elevated diction and formal syntax and the desires expressed. Notice the lack of contractions, the use of constructions like "I hope" and "I pray" and the Latinate diction like "advances" and "overtures" contrasting with the image of the speaker and her beloved being showered with fruit—and babies—by monkeys! The equivalence of fruit and babies I find particularly funny—the fruit is bruised, but the babies are unharmed. This vision of paradise is entirely new. My favorite moment in the poem is an aural awakening: the sound of the words, "with a delicate snap, like a rice cracker." Those words, allied to the image of the deliciously light cracker, change the "obstacle" before our very eyes: we see and hear the obstacle being reduced to something frivolous, capable of being held in the fingers and snapped by the teeth. The rhetorical situations of Gerstler's poems are clear and even conventional, but her language is fresh and surprising.

Another example of a tone I admire appears in a poem by Gerstler that pokes fun at Elizabeth Bishop's "One Art," or rather, our culture's reification of Bishop's poem:

*The Story of Toasted Cheese*

> *Toasted cheese hath no master.*
> —a proverb

Toasted cheese hath no master.
Streams of priests running
from pink bungalows faster
and faster were seen reading
*The Fronds of God,*

prophesying disaster.
Indoors, toddlers munched crumbs
of ancient wall plaster.
You slapped her for calling Dad
a "majestic bastard"?
At the mouth of a sacred cave,
kneeling in gravel, he asked her.
The ostrich race will take place
in that picturesque cow pasture.
Will you have oysters Rockefeller
now to begin your repast, sir?
Her premonition consisted
of "seeing" her dear sister
romanced by a sandblaster.
Monique loved the rough, comforting
hum of that scruffy black cat's purr.
The botanist finally recognized
(tears filling her overworked eyes)
a rare, blue, Chinese aster.[26]

Look at how the poem echoes Bishop's rhyme scheme but then becomes wilder and wilder in its rhymes: *disaster / master / cow pasture / repast, sir?* It suggests a runaway train. What holds the poem together is its very lack of unity, as if in response to Bishop's complete control. The poem is brilliant in its silliness, in the way not one line is close to iambic and in the way it starts with toasted cheese and ends with an aster. Like Gertrude Stein's spearing of Marinetti in her poem "Marry Nettie," Gerstler makes fun by relying on her audience's acuity. Gerstler chooses the "low" subject of toasted cheese to contrast with Bishop's "high" subjects of art and loss. We praise Elizabeth Bishop's poem for its perfection, for the way the details hold together and appear seamless, but this poem is the postmodern response: the center cannot hold, and it's a sham to pretend that it does.

Of the five poets mentioned here, Brenda Shaughnessy is the one who most shares Gertrude Stein's love of wordplay. Shaughnessy's book of love poems, *Interior with Sudden Joy,* employs linguistic surprise, often alongside the categories of surprise mentioned above. Shaughnessy mines the dictionary in order to reinvent it. Her method of surprise functions like a template placed over our expectations, producing poems rife with inversions, puns, and game-playing. Here are two stanzas from her poem "Your One Good Dress":

> . . . And the red dress (think about it,
> redress) is all neckhole. The brown
> is a big wet beard with, of course, a backslit.
> You're only as sick as your secrets.
> There is an argument for the dull-chic,
> the dirty olive and the Cinderelly. But those
> who exhort it are only part of the conspiracy:
> "Shimmer, shmimmer," they'll say. "Lush, shmush."[27]

In these stanzas and those that follow, the description of the dress holds the poem together and keeps the reader from getting lost, but Shaughnessy takes that dress and flies with it. There is something childishly charming about the puns and wordplay here: the pun on "redress," the characterization of the other dresses, the "Cinderelly" dull-chic. In another stanza, the serious directive "Bury your children in it" followed by the adolescent "Visit your pokey hometown friends in it." My favorite surprising moment in the poem, however, is the list of Columbus' ships, which I transform in my mind into dresses, their masts and flags flying.

> Am I now. You put on your Nina, your Pinta, your
> Santa Maria. Make it simple to last your whole
> life long. Make it black. Glassy or deep.
> Your body is opium and you are its only true smoker.[28]

"Make it simple to last your whole life long" is a line from a song ("Sing"), by Joseph Raposo, the musical director of *Sesame Street*.[29] The juxtaposition of Columbus' ships next to a saccharine line from a popular song is an unexpected juxtaposition. In retrospect, what makes me "buy it," rather than dismiss it, is that both images have the long-standing quality Shaughnessy is revering in the dress.

I have mentioned a mere handful of moments in the work of a handful of Stein's granddaughters, but I could as easily have discussed the poetry of, to name a few more, Anne Carson, Lynn Emanuel, Stefanie Marlis, Heather McHugh, Molly McQuade, Harryette Mullen, Laura Mullen, Judith Taylor, and C. D. Wright. But in this mere handful of poems, the element of surprise has challenged our assumptions: about what will happen a hundred years hence, about the nature of hands, about the essence of the good black dress. We live in a world of default assumptions: nothing we do—nothing we say, eat, drink, buy, or make—is free of them. It takes unconventional thinking, perhaps even genius, to make and break free.

*Notes*

1. Robert Bly, *Leaping Poetry: An Idea with Poems and Translations* (Boston: Beacon, 1972), 1.

2. Antonio Damasio, *Descartes' Error: Emotion, Reason, and the Human Brain* (New York: Avon, 1995).

3. Marjorie Perloff, *Wittgenstein's Ladder: Poetic Language and the Strangeness of the Ordinary* (Chicago: University of Chicago Press, 1996), 88–89.

4. Gertrude Stein, *The Yale Gertrude Stein*, ed. Richard Kostelanetz (New Haven: Yale University Press, 1980), 26.

5. Immanuel Kant, *Critique of Judgement* (Oxford: Oxford University Press, 1997).

6. Roman Jakobson and Krystyna Pomorsk, *Dialogues*, trans. Christian Hubert (Cambridge: MIT Press, 1983); Roman Jakobson, *Verbal Art, Verbal Sign, Verbal Time*, ed. Krystyna Pomorska and Stephen Rudy (Minneapolis: University of Minneapolis Press, 1985); Roman Jakobson and Linda Waugh, *The Sound Shape of Language* (Bloomington: Indiana University Press, 1979).

7. Susan Stewart, *Nonsense* (Baltimore: Johns Hopkins University Press, 1978).

8. Octavio Paz, *The Other Voice* (New York: Harcourt Brace & Jovanovich, 1990), 9.

9. John Morreall, "A New Theory of Laughter," *Philosophical Studies* 42 (1982), 249.

10. *Encyclopedia of Psychology*, 2nd ed., vol. 3, ed. Raymond Corsini (New York: John Wiley & Sons, 1994), 495.

11. *Encyclopedia of Psychology*, 495.

12. *Encyclopedia of Psychology*, 495.

13. Wulf-Uwe Meyer et al, "An Experimental Analysis of Surprise," *Cognition and Emotion* 5, no. 4 (1991).

14. Amittai Avivram, e-mail message to Natasha Sajé, October 1998.

15. Stein, *The Yale Gertrude Stein*, 121.

16. Gertrude Stein, *Selected Writings of Gertrude Stein,* ed. Carl Van Vechten (New York: Vintage, 1972), 515.

17. Jeanne Marie Beaumont, "The Valley of My Attentions," in *Placebo Effects* (New York: Norton, 1997), 1.

18. Mary Ruefle, "The Cart," in *Cold Pluto* (Pittsburgh: Carnegie Mellon University Press, 1996), 48. Reprinted with permission of the author.

19. Andre Breton, "First Manifesto of Surrealism—1924," Poetry in Translation, August 31, 2012, http://www.poetryintranslation.com/PITBR/French/Manifesto.htm.

20. Mary Ruefle, "Tilapia," in *Post Meridian* (Pittsburgh: Carnegie Mellon University Press, 2000), 64. Reprinted with permission of the author.

21. Belle Waring, "Look," in *Dark Blonde* (Louisville: Sarabande, 1997), 5.

22. Belle Waring, "Use the Following Construction in a Sentence," in *Dark Blonde*, 16.

23. Jeanne Marie Beaumont, "Excavation," in *Placebo Effects*, 65. Used by permission of W.W. Norton & Company, Inc.

24. Mikhail Bakhtin, *The Dialogic Imagination,* ed. Michael Holquist, trans. Caryl Emerson and Michael Holquist (Austin: University of Texas Press, 1981).

25. Amy Gerstler, "Request," in *Crown of Weeds* (New York: Penguin, 1997), 23.

26. Amy Gerstler, "The Story of Toasted Cheese," in *Medicine* (New York: Penguin, 2000), 11. Used by permission of Penguin, a division of Penguin Group (USA) LLC.

27. Brenda Shaughnessy, "Your One Good Dress," in *Interior with Sudden Joy* (New York: Farrar, Straus & Giroux, 1999), 30.

28. Shaughnessy, *Interior with Sudden Joy*, 30.

29. Joseph Raposo, "Sing," Risa Song Lyrics Archive, August 31, 2012, http://www.guntheranderson.com/v/data/sing.htm.

# Metonymy, the Neglected
# (but Necessary) Trope

Medieval rhetorician Peter Ramus lists only four important tropes: metaphor, metonymy, synecdoche (a part for the whole, which later commentators subsume into metonymy), and irony.[1] Metaphor has received by far the most critical attention, and is also the trope most closely connected with poetry, as for example in Percy Shelley's observation that "the language of poets is vitally metaphorical."[2] At the time (June 2013) I am revising this essay, the search terms "metaphor and poetry" yield 2,685 hits in the Modern Language Association bibliography, while "metonymy and poetry" result in only 173. Indeed, I've never seen an essay about metonymy for an audience of poets, possibly because that trope is so poorly understood, despite its enduring importance.

In simple terms, *metaphor* (Greek, "to carry through") refers to comparison, while *metonymy* (Greek, "through the name") refers to substitution. Because all nouns "substitute" for the things they name and are therefore metonyms, most poems contain some element of metonymy. When a poem names a person or place or a date, we might recognize that a substitution is taking place, simply because the poet has chosen a specific detail over others.

Some poets favor metaphor over metonymy—Paul Celan, Louise Glück, Eugenio Montale, and Franz Wright, for example. Metaphor makes their poems seem universal and timeless, primarily because they aren't anchored in time and place. For instance, in Stanley Plumly's poem "The Marriage in the Trees" a marriage is compared, via extended metaphor, to a series of trees.[3] One of the sophisticated aspects of the poem is the way the marriage is compared not to one particular tree, but to a series, signifying marriage as a live entity rather than a static thing, an entity that must change form if it is to survive the years. Marriage is not "like" trees as much as it is "*in* trees." The poem favors metaphor over metonymy because the *comparison* of the marriage to trees is more important than naming trees, persons, or stating dates and places.

But perhaps trying for timelessness is a fool's errand. When a poem is more *metonymic*, it admits its partial status, the writer choosing one detail out of many to represent the object or person, just as a culture chooses which things are important by naming, producing, and reproducing them. Generally these reproductions reinforce existing hierarchies of power, as when, for instance, we refer to a photocopy machine as a Xerox even if that is not its manufacturer.

I've heard many poets denigrate poems containing proper nouns on the grounds that specificity in a poem prevents it being "universal." Take, for example, the diary-like poems of Frank O'Hara, anchored in particular time, place, and objects. Relying less on image and metaphor and more on metonymy, they are infused with the detail of a particular life. They "date" themselves, literally, in the way eighteenth-century poets John Dryden and Alexander Pope date themselves by addressing particular political issues and by using names. "The Day Lady Died"[4] could not be written today, a good thing because the poem exists also as history.

Because metonymic poems do not presume to be "universal," they do not scorn pop culture or "low" references. Thus a critic like Richard Ohmann wonders if using product brand names turns a poem into advertising.[5] Is there a way to see the substitution of a brand name for a generic in a positive light—as a metonym fixing the poem in time and place, not necessarily something that reduces the poem's value? Harryette Mullen's poem "Dim Lady" is a metonymic transcription of Shakespeare's Sonnet 130. "My mistress's eyes are nothing like the sun" becomes "My honeybunch's peepers are nothing like neon." By updating the diction and incorporating proper nouns such as "Red Lobster," "Liquid Paper," "Slinkys," Muzak," and "Marilyn Monroes," Mullen emphasizes the effect of capitalism on language—and love. Four hundred years after Shakespeare, the nouns "roses," "sun," "perfume," and "music" sound generic to ears attuned to the multiplicity of products created by capitalism. And today, the word "mistress" suggests government officials caught in illicit affairs, while "honeybunch" is a slang term of endearment, albeit one that may no longer be used fifty years from now.[6]

While writers can surprise us with new metaphorical comparisons, metonymy relies on attributes we already assume to be true. Thus metonymy deals with interrelationships of things (by transfer or renaming), condenses habitual relationships (shorthand), and offers a plethora of data that we would unite into one meaning. Metonymic poems are not always easy to read because proper nouns often demand research. A hundred years from now, for example, readers might have to look up "Kleenex," or for that matter, "tissue." Language changes, and poets should not try to prevent that change, but poets who exploit what is vitally metonymic are acknowledging history, calling attention to the temporality of all language.

In what follows I will braid together two threads of inquiry about language. The first thread—I'll call it *structural*—begins with the ancients' categorization of figurative language, and is expanded upon by Russian formalist Roman Jakobson, who in 1956 argued a binary opposition between metaphor and metonymy, a distinction based on dominance.[7] David Lodge's book *The Modes of Modern Writing: Metaphor, Metonymy, and the Typology of Modern Literature* builds on Jakobson's insights and its reliance on structuralist thinking.[8]

The second thread—call it *poststructural*—has roots in Friedrich Nietzsche's philosophy (circa 1870s), in his insight that all language is constructed, and that all naming constitutes a kind of violence:

> What then is truth? A mobile army of metaphors, metonyms, anthropomorphisms, a sum, in short, of human relationships which, rhetorically and poetically intensified, ornamented, and transformed, come to be thought of, after long usage by people, as fixed, binding, and canonical. Truths are illusions whose illusionary nature has been forgotten, metaphors that have been used up and lost their imprint and that now operate as mere metal, no longer as coins.[9]

Nouns, both concrete and abstract, are constructions that are often not recognized as such. Nietzsche understood that language is neither fixed nor solid, but rather reflects and creates the values of the culture using the language. Nietzsche would say that a word has no "proper" or stable meaning—it is always in flux. Jacques Lacan built on this assumption *and* the opposition between metonymy and metaphor outlined by the formalist Jakobson, arguing that metonymy is "the signifier of desire," representing endless postponement and deferral. In other words, we name things and write about them because we don't have them.[10]

There are linguists—George Lakoff, Mark Turner, and Mark Johnson, for example—who use both of the above threads of inquiry about language.[11] Arguing that metaphor and metonymy are pervasive, they categorize typical metaphors ("Life is a journey," "An argument is a war," "Ideas are food") to show that all language—not just poetry—relies on them. In short, figurative language not only represents, but also helps to create, cultural assumptions.

In part II of his book *Fundamentals of Language*, "Two Aspects of Language and Two Types of Aphasic Disturbances," Roman Jakobson outlines the differences between metaphor and metonymy by examining two kinds of aphasia, a severe speech disability. In the first kind, termed "similarity disorder," the aphasic might say "fork" for "knife" or "table" for "lamp" or "smoke" for "pipe." In struggling with this disability, the context allows the patient to supply similar words. This patient understands language *only* through metonymy, through substitutions.

The other kind of aphasia, a "contiguity disorder," diminishes the extent and variety of sentences so that "the syntactical rules organizing words into a higher unit are lost."[12] The patient suffering then has trouble with connections—with grammar—and therefore would be unable to play the game Dictionary, wherein players are asked to provide or guess plausible meanings for imaginary words. Such a patient would provide a word that shares no context with the prompt. As David Lodge points out, postmodern literature, for instance the work of Samuel Beckett and Gertrude Stein, contains examples of this type. A prose poem from Stein's *Tender Buttons*, serves as an example:

> Rhubarb is susan not susan not seat in bunch toys not wild
> and laughable not in little places not in neglect and veg-
> etable not in fold coal age not please.[13]

There is nothing (except perhaps the word "vegetable") in the poem that we would "normally" associate with the rhubarb plant, say its red stem, its poisonous leaves, its sour taste, its use in pies. "Susan" is a word normally unassociated with "rhubarb."

The "metaphoric and metonymic poles," as Jakobson terms them, run through many kinds of verbal exchange, including "free association." To the word "hut," some people might respond "burned out," while others might say "poor little house."[14] Romanticism and Symbolism are supported by metaphor, while the epic tends to be grounded in metonymy.

Realist fiction has always been allied with metonymy, because novels are "world-creating," and a large part of this creation is due to names, places, and times that could be "real." Growing as it does out of journalism, travel writing, and autobiography, the genre of the novel mimics all three of them. Many critics have studied the metonymies of particular novelists. As for drama, the critic David Lodge expands on the two poles of metaphor and metonymy and argues that drama is inherently metaphorical (because a variety of actors can play the same part), while film is metonymic (because of its emphasis on close-up).

In Frazer's *The Golden Bough*, two kinds of magic clarify the difference between the two poles of metaphor and metonymy. Metaphoric magic involves making an effigy of the person one desires, while metonymic magic involves taking some of the person's hair (or a piece of clothing) for a spell. In metonymy one thing *indicates* another—the hair *represents* the person.[15]

When we say, "Ships plowed the sea," we are making a metaphorical comparison between the keel of a ship and a plow that goes through earth; there is no context between plow and ships. When we say, "Keels crossed the sea," on the other hand, we are using a part of the ship (the keel) to represent the whole—metonymy. Interestingly, sometimes metonyms are actually buried in the metaphor. For instance, when we say, "He's shooting his mouth off," the word "mouth" stands in for the faculty of speech, while the comparison between using a gun and foolish talk is a metaphor.

The more metaphoric a text is, the more likely it is to be labeled "literature," creating a continuum, with highly metonymic newspapers at one end and poems at the other, a continuum often used by poets to increase their standing as artists (and "*not* journalists"). I am most interested, however, in what Jakobson would term the "line of greatest resistance,"[16] poems that resemble newspapers or encyclopedias in their use of metonymy.

Metonymy shows us how we (are taught to) see the world through the things we connect and represent. And so it is that an analysis of metonymy involves understanding part-whole relationships, as well as contexts and categories. All nouns and pronouns are metonyms because they stand in for what they signify. Prepositions are important in identifying metonyms because they indicate the kind of substitution: for example, "in" indicates place, while "as" or "for" indicates a person in a playbill. The abundance of nouns in modern poetry reflects the proliferation of manufactured things. Rather than trying to ignore this trend, I believe we should analyze it.

We can think of metonymy as a political force, and there are two ways we might go about that thinking. On the one hand, like metaphor, metonymy works unobtrusively and does not explain the associations it relies upon. In other words, the metaphor "Life is a journey" is so common that it is taken for granted as true. Similarly, when we say (metonymically) "Mrs. John Smith," the fact that the husband's name is substituted for the wife's is also taken for granted. In the case of both the metaphor and the metonym above, the default association is patriarchal—an association so pervasive it needs no explanation. Note that metonymy, even more so than metaphor, is difficult to detach and decode. Metonymy identifies an invisible quality (such as wealth) by a visible exterior such as a Hermès handbag. But we are so used to processing metonyms we don't recognize them as such.

When I say that "I'm reading Emily Dickinson," I'm substituting the producer for the product, a substitution that seems "natural" in 2013. However, this substitution points to the creation of the author as an individual, something that happened mostly after the Renaissance in English literature. The Middle Ages put far less emphasis on individual authors and their "name recognition." By using the metonym that substitutes an author's name for his or her work, we are reinforcing the cult of the author. When we say, "America is a powerful country," we are substituting the whole North and South American continent for the country of the United States, a substitution that reveals the dominance of the United States in the minds of its citizens. Similarly, when we say, "Let's drink champagne," we are substituting the particular (produced in a very specific region of France) for the generic, sparkling wine—which is like "Give me my java," a substitution of a place in Indonesia for a product grown there. When we say, "The buses are on strike," we are substituting the object for the user, a dehumanizing gesture. When I say, "I have to grade papers this weekend," the action of assigning the grade (sadly) substitutes for the whole process of reading and evaluating student work because it is the grade that is valued most by students and the system.

Metonyms also access history. Some proper names—Smith and Miller, for example—were originally metonyms standing in for occupations. Even though they don't function as stand-ins anymore, they should still remind us of the formation of metonyms and their historical importance. Is 9/11 a metonym for "the terror attacks that destroyed the World Trade Center towers and struck the Pentagon"? The date and its pleasing rhythm make for convenient shorthand. One could also say "the 2001 terrorist attacks" or "the events of September 11, 2001," but "9/11" also echoes the emergency telephone number, 911, which I think is why, along with brevity, it became the preferred metonym. But not every metonym functions as a noun in the sentence. When I say, "I'm going to shampoo my hair," the instrument is substituted for the action because the product is so commonly used in an action—cleaning the hair.

We can point to Dante, and also to most eighteenth-century poets, as leaning more to the metonym than to the metaphor. When it comes to contemporary poets, some poets who come to mind are Wanda Coleman, Denise Duhamel, Albert Goldbarth, Jorie Graham, Tony Hoagland, Campbell McGrath, Paul Mul-

doon, Tracy K. Smith, and David Wojahn. David Lodge reads
Philip Larkin as an antimodernist poet whose work is more met-
onymic than metaphoric, an "experimental" literary gesture on
Larkin's part.

But in the case of contemporary U.S. poets, I believe the
metonymic preference is actually allied to an interest in—and
a commitment to—history and/or an examination of contem-
porary culture. I would argue that, unlike metaphor, metonymy
shuns false certainties and emphasizes process via the play of
associations. Proper nouns in particular call attention to the his-
torical context that creates them. The following poem by Judith
Hall exemplifies how names and roles substitute for persons,
and how nicknames substitute for names, while also exemplify-
ing the role of women as (literally) sex objects.

Upon the Bed-Trick Played on Jack

> Why, all the souls that were were forfeit once.
> —*Measure for Measure*, 2.2

MARILYN [*as* ISABELLA]: *I had rather give my body than my soul*—
      [*as* MARILYN]: Some lines come more easily than others.

> I read this to Jack over the telephone.
> Exhale on "my"? Inhale "body"?
>     Hundreds,
>
> He had a thousand comic "vigorous"
>     breaths
> To recommend . . . for *me*, as Isabella,
>
> Dear nun! Frigid, misfit, desperate.

[*as* NORMA JEAN]: I know her, know the dream that God—
      absent

> God alone—loves me—*God, I wanted to
> learn!*

    [*as* MARILYN]: Why did he laugh? Finally, they all laugh.
    [*as* ISABELLA]: "I had rather—" drain off memories, if
      mercy

[*as* MARILYN]: Is defined as high colonics. . . . or
champagne

Or servicing the presidential prick?
[*as* ISABELLA]: The rest—the soul rumored into farce—
predicted.

\*

JOHN [*as* JACK]: God, her ass, a veritable New Fron—tée—
ah!
*She* in town—then Jackie "insists" we catch
*Meh-shah fah Meh-shah* . . .
Fun as Communion; we took it from rank
bastards
Who spent their nights rejoicing at the
baths.

[*as* ANGELO]: *And she will speak most bitterly and strange.*

[*as* PRESIDENT]: I remember. The one about a great man's
failings.
Absurd deceptions, in the name of
romance.

[*as* JOHN]: I constructed romances on a man's
health,
On "vigah" from amphetamines and
cortisone.
The pain—my own parzody of faith—
Was used to humanize me: God's good
sport
Reduced to ergonomic rocking chairs.
She asked other men to throw my son in
the air.

\*

JACQUELINE [*as* MARIANA]: *I have known my husband, yet my husband*
*Knows not that ever he knew me.*
[*as* JACQUELINE]: For I was Marilyn, when Marilyn
Cooed his "happy-ever-aftering."

94

[ *as* JACKIE]:  His sadly perfunctory rhapsodies were
                    rude,
[ *as* JACQUELINE]:  Were all the same to me, since I was
                    always
                    Mary, Angie, Grace, Giancana's Judith,
                    His growing underclass of compulsive
                    lays.

Liquor, lighting, hand-painted Paris
    scarves
Mattered more, in a husband's education,
Than any woman's luscious incarnation.

Oscar Wilde: "To become the spectator
Of one's own life is to escape the
    suffering . . ."
I tried, Love, and Damn, but love
    survived.[17]

Hall's poem consists of three sonnets, spoken in the voice of
Marilyn Monroe, John F. Kennedy, and Jacqueline Kennedy.
The poem relies on the Shakespeare play *Measure for Measure*.
Isabella is a nun who uses a bed trick to save her brother Clau-
dio from being executed for having sex with his betrothed. The
(good) Duke disguises himself as a friar to observe what hap-
pens when the other (evil) ruler Angelo is in charge. Angelo
offers to commute Claudio's sentence if Isabella will sleep with
him; Angelo himself was betrothed to Mariana but called off
the marriage when her dowry was lost in a shipwreck. In the
end, Mariana pretends to be Isabella and sleeps with Angelo,
while Isabella is "married off" to the Duke. Her silence at the
end is interpreted as consent. Modern commentators find the
play problematic and no longer classify it as a comedy, as it was
in the First Folio.

In Hall's poem, Marilyn Monroe "acts" the part of Isabella,
the nun; John Kennedy is the manipulative ruler Angelo; and
Jacqueline Kennedy is Marianna, his cast-aside betrothed. The
substitution of a play for an imagined scene in history is itself
a *metonym*, and the realm of the theater highlights metonymy.
In the poem, people act as characters in a play but also as dif-

ferent versions of themselves. Names are metonyms that reveal cultural roles and values. Norma Jean Baker is the birth name of a woman who took the screen name of Marilyn Monroe; John Fitzgerald Kennedy was also known as JFK, John, Jack, and Mr. President (most famously in a birthday song sung by Marilyn Monroe); Jacqueline Bouvier became Jacqueline Kennedy when she married but she was also known by the nickname "Jackie." The similarity of Jack and Jackie provides another level of metonymic interest, and the First Lady can often substitute for the president in relatively insignificant social situations (funerals, for instance). The issue of naming foregrounds the question: Who is—and when do we get to see—the "real" person? Hall's poem enacts Lacan's notion that metonymy is an endless signifier of desire. The myriad substitutions in the poem point to the impossibility of any person ever being outside a role, outside a name. The Hollywood "head shot," as David Lodge points out, is a metonym: the image substitutes for the person.

On one level, the fact that Jack is tricked into sleeping with his own wife instead of Marilyn Monroe suggests a feminist reversal. Cut off from real power, women gain power by playing tricks. However, the play also suggests that sexually, women are interchangeable to men. JFK also has sex with Mary, Angie, Grace, and Giancana's Judith (a group wittily referred to as a "growing underclass"). In Renaissance drama the bed trick is sometimes interrogated and debated as a form of rape—of the *man*. Jack gets what he deserves because his power, like Angelo's, is hypocritical and misused. His "new frontier"—a grand plan— is reduced to a woman's "ass." Another metonym in the poem is the substitution of "other men" for Jack because his back injury prevents him from tossing his children in the air.

The poem abounds in references to Catholicism, which itself is a host (pun intended) of metonymies. The host substitutes for the body of Christ, for instance, and the priest for God. John F. Kennedy, of course, was the first Catholic president, who in the poem becomes "the presidential prick" to be serviced. In Catholicism, priests function as metonyms for God, and in the confessional, both the identity of the confessor and the priest are masked, at least in theory. The speech of the confession and the speech of prayer absolve whatever sin has been committed. I can't help but think of Foucault's *History of Sexuality*, in which he points out that in the twentieth century, the speech of psychoanalysis replaces the speech of the confessional.[18] In both cases, speaking about an act substitutes for the act, providing pleasure or absolution or both. In the poem, mercy becomes champagne which then changes into high colonics, surely a pun on "high mass" as well as a reference to the practice of colon cleansing popular among film stars. If Hollywood (itself a metonym for the film industry) emphasizes the body, then Catholicism is supposed to emphasize the soul.

The last stanza of the poem alludes to Jacqueline Kennedy's stated affinity for the writings of Oscar Wilde. The last line resists easy summary: "I tried, Love, and Damn, but love survived" can be read in the following ways:

> I tried to dismiss you, Jack, but I couldn't.
> I tested the abstraction of Love but it resisted me.
> I tried both love and damnation, and love survived.

A Renaissance nun would have vowed chastity to God with her body erased from the transaction; Norma Jean Baker in her fealty to Hollywood makes her body the most important part of the contract. Hers was a body appreciated not only by Hollywood but also by powerful men in sports (Joe DiMaggio), literature (Arthur Miller), and Washington (JFK). Monroe lifted weights to stay in shape; JFK took amphetamines and cortisone to try to. JFK was fairly successful in hiding his body's disability from the world, while Marilyn Monroe was required to expose her body's ability (think of the publicity photograph from *Some Like It Hot* which "accidentally" exposes her legs over a subway grate).

Has women's status changed in three hundred years? I think the poem argues that it has not. Moreover, the poem comments on the power of the ruler to alter the lives of others. Angelo, the Duke, and JFK all have power over others because of their status. One wonders if Marilyn Monroe would have preferred to say no. Through its metonymies this poem highlights the probationary status of names. Names and titles are dependent on circumstances; they change. The reader cannot help but pay attention to the different positions of the speakers as their contexts determine their fate. There is no universal truth to be gleaned from the poem; rather, as Jill Matus notes: "Metonymies are neither definitive nor absolute; they suspend sentence and make every formulation a probation."[19] Furthermore, metonyms highlight positionality, blindness about which "is the basis of many cultural and environmental problems: class, race, women in patriarchal culture." In other words, the very specificity of the references in the poem asks readers to question the power relationships that created those substitutions. In this poem, metonymy is a trope that interrogates patriarchy and heterosexism.

Another poem that not only uses metonymy but can also be said to be "about" the trope itself is Lucia Perillo's "The Oldest Map with the Name America."[20] In and of itself, a map highlights metonymy, because what we call something impacts how we see it, and vice versa. In the first and third stanza of her poem, Perillo comments on the practice of inexact mapmaking, and more generally on the practice of naming, due to an incomplete or inaccurate point of view—which in turn leads to the insight that every point of view is incomplete. In between, Perillo places the second stanza, which situates the speaker as a child learning that her world, bounded by the end of the street, was incomplete, and moreover that the infinity of the larger world beyond the woodlot frightened her: "when you fall down there, you fall forever." No longer safe in her basement with her "thingmaker" making things out of "plasticgoop," the speaker must confront a rimless world.

Making language substitutes for making things. Metonymy is in force not only in material objects, but also in the way we *see* "the natural world." What we name shows what we value. But leaving *out* what we don't know is another option, ancillary to pretending it doesn't exist. Like a cat who thinks he is hidden when only his head is under the bed, a young child cannot imagine anything other than his own point of view and limitations. Perillo's poem underscores the way that metonymy is dependent on context. Remarkably, the poem ends with the metonym "cannibals"—humans who eat humans, who do not think their practice is noteworthy enough to warrant a label.

Susan Howe's "Melville's Marginalia" offers another example of metonymy, also grounded in historical point of view. The poem begins with a chronology of James Clarence Mangan, 1803–1849, an Irish poet and clerk whom Howe believes is the inspiration for Herman Melville's "Bartleby the Scrivener." Howe tells of happening upon a doctoral work, "Melville's Marginalia," by Wilson Walker Cohen (who received his degree from Harvard in 1965):

> Names who are strangers out of bounds out of the bound margin: I thought one way to write about a loved author would be to follow what trails he follows through the words of others: what if these penciled single double and triple scorings arrows short phrases angry outbursts crosses cryptic ciphers sudden enthusiasms mysterious erasures have come to find you too here again, now.[21]

Howe not only takes pleasure in documenting the link between James Clarence Mangan and Melville, but also makes us completely aware that fictional representations are metonyms that relate to the "real world." She tells us that her method of writing the poem was "free association" and that "poetry is thought transference."[22] Howe substitutes her own life and writing for those of Melville and Mangan: "Free association isn't free." Language and character are transmuted through the metonyms—all of history, including literary history, is accessed through names. Howe's poem is partly an elegy for the now forgotten Mangan: "Three persons are said to / have followed his remains / to the grave."[23] The metonyms here—persons, remains, and grave—have a sadly elegiac tone. Their names are not known, and neither would Mangan's be, without Howe.

The irony of Melville's current fame and his obscurity during his lifetime, and Cohen's young death, also reflects on the nature of what is known, when, and how. "Print settles it," Howe tells us on the last page, "print is sentinel." Presumably, the fact that Melville's books were printed, however obscure, allowed him to be rediscovered, as was Mangan by Howe. The title of the whole collection, of which "Melville's Marginalia" is the final and (according to the back cover) "essential"—poem, is *The Nonconformist's Memorial.* A writer can honor another only by mentioning him by name, by anchoring him in history. Like nonfiction, Howe's poem is abundant with information—names, dates, places, and sources. And like Anne Carson, who also combines poetry and prose in literary criticism, and also honors other writers via metonymy, Howe's poetry is in relief against the prose.

Metonymic poems combine well with other genres, for instance biography, journalism, or film, and they exist across a wide range of poetic styles, as I hope I have suggested by my examples. Metonymic poems do not hold themselves "above" other genres or the culture that produced them. As Fredric Jameson points out in *Postmodernism, or The Logic of Late Capitalism,* blended and blurred genres signal the insecurities and freedoms of consumer society, the dismantling of distinctions between high art and low.[24] No, poetry is not journalism, but neither is it free of the culture that produces it. In fact, to keep it alive and well, and to remind us that the world changes and values are not universal, poetry *needs* the nouns that place us firmly into history, even into our roles as consumers. Metonyms help us understand what we take for granted and metonymic poems critique our culture, something as sorely necessary today as it was in the eighteenth century. As Gertrude Stein wrote, "Poetry is doing nothing but losing refusing and pleasing and betraying and caressing nouns."[25]

*Notes*

1. Chaim Perelman and Lucie Olbrechts-Tyteca, *The New Rhetoric: A Treatise on Argumentation,* trans. John Wilkinson and Purcell Weaver (Notre Dame: University of Notre Dame Press, 1969).

2. Percy Bysshe Shelley, "A Defence of Poetry," *Bartleby: Great Books Online,* August 31, 2012, http://www.bartleby.com/27/23.html.

3. Stanley Plumly, "The Marriage in the Trees," in *Now That My Fa-*

*ther Lies Down Beside Me: New and Selected Poems, 1970–2000* (New York: Ecco, 2001).

4. Frank O' Hara, "The Day Lady Died," Poetry Foundation, August 31, 2012, http://www.poetryfoundation.org/poem/171368.

5. Richard Ohmann, "Teaching Historically," in *Politics of Knowledge: The Commercialization of the University, the Professions, and Print Culture* (Middletown, CT: Wesleyan University Press, 2003).

6. Harryette Mullen, "Dim Lady," in *Sleeping with the Dictionary* (Berkeley: University of California Press, 2002.)

7. Roman Jakobson, "Two Aspects of Language and Two Types of Linguistic Disturbances," in *Fundamentals of Language*, by Roman Jakobson and Morris Halle (The Hague: Mouton, 1956).

8. David Lodge, *The Modes of Modern Writing: Metaphor, Metonymy, and the Typology of Modern Literature* (Ithaca: Cornell University Press, 1977).

9. Friedrich Nietzsche, "On Truth and Lies in a Nonmoral Sense," in *Everyday Theory*, ed. Becky Renee McLaughlin and Bob Coleman (New York: Pearson/Longman, 2005), 753.

10. Jacques Lacan, "The Instance of the Letter in the Unconscious," in *Écrits: A Selection*, trans. Bruce Fink (New York: Norton, 2002).

11. George Lakoff and Mark Johnson, *Metaphors We Live By* (Chicago, University of Chicago Press, 1980).

12. Jakobson, "Two Aspects of Language," 71.

13. Gertrude Stein, "RHUBARB," in *Tender Buttons* (Sioux Falls: NuVision Publications LE, 2007), 32.

14. Jakobson, "Two Aspects of Language," 77.

15. James Frazer, "The Golden Bough," *Bartleby: Great Books Online*, August 31, 2012, http://www.bartleby.com/196/.

16. Jakobson, "Two Aspects of Language," 82.

17. Judith Hall, "Upon the Bed-Trick Played on Jack," in *The Promised Folly* (Evanston: Triquarterly Press, 2003), 19–20. Copyright 2003 by Judith Hall. Published by TriQuarterly Books / Northwestern University Press. All Rights Reserved.

18. Michel Foucault, *The History of Sexuality, vol. 1, An Introduction*, trans. Robert Hurley (New York: Random House, 1978).

19. Jill Matus, "Proxy and Proximity: Metonymic Signing," *University of Toronto Quarterly* 58, no. 2 (Winter 1988–99), 310.

20. Lucia Perillo, *The Oldest Map with the Name America* (New York: Random House, 1999), 119–121.

21. Susan Howe, "Melville's Marginalia," in *The NonConformist's Memorial* (New York: New Directions, 1993), 92.

22. Howe, "Melville's Marginalia," 105.

23. Howe, "Melville's Marginalia," 138.

24. Fredric Jameson, *Postmodernism, or the Cultural Logic of Late Capitalism* (Durham, NC: Duke University Press, 1991).

25. Gertrude Stein, "Poetry and Grammar," in *Lectures in America* (New York: Random House, 1935).

# "Why Must It Always End This Way?"

## *Narrative Poetry and Its (Dis)contents*

There are four modes of poetry—story (narrative), song (lyric), description, and argument. We know that individual poems may combine these modes. An epic narrative, for example, contains description, and a lyric refrain may have an embedded argument. And yet it seems that poets have placed *narrative* in binary opposition to *lyric*—or at least they have for the past thirty years or so in the United States. Moreover, like most binary oppositions, the opposition of narrative to lyric is politically charged. It's important that both the contemporary poet and the reader of poetry understand why this is so.

But before we can even begin to understand the argument against narrative in poetry, we need to understand what narrative *is*.

A narrative structure can occur in any literary genre, including poetry. Again, etymology points us in the right direction. "Narrative" has its roots in an ancient word meaning "to know." Narrators tell us what they know, an obvious insight that signals the limitations of any story. Another way to define narrative is through *change*: when a situation changes, it creates a plot. As the French literary theorist Gérard Genette tells us, there is story "as soon as there is an action or an event, even a single one," the reason being that "there is a transformation, a transition from an earlier state to a later and resultant state."[1] In other words, "story" refers to the totality of narrated events, while "narrative" is the discourse—oral or written—that *narrates* the events. In the French the distinction is made with the terms *histoire* and *récit*.

Theorist J. Hillis Miller defines narrative as having three elements: personification, plot, and patterning.[2] Personification involves a *protagonist* (who wants something), an *antagonist* (who prevents the protagonist from getting what he wants), and a *witness* who learns. In a poem, it may be that one character may serve all three of these elements. For example, in Elizabeth Bishop's "The Fish,"[3] we can say that the speaker is the protagonist (who wants the fish), *and* the antagonist (who wants to let it go), *and* the witness who learns. We know that many satisfying stories result from a protagonist/antagonist with an *internal* struggle—two forces "warring" within one character.

The second element—plot—also consists of three parts: an *initial situation*, followed by a sequence leading to a *change* or reversal of that situation, and a *revelation* made possible by the change. If we look again at Bishop's "The Fish," we can say that the initial situation is that the speaker has caught a big fish, and that the sequence leading to a change is the speaker's examination of (and growing respect for) the body of the fish—including the hooks in his mouth and wallpaper-like skin and barnacles—all of which results in her throwing the fish back. Finally we can say that the revelation of the poem is expressed in the penultimate line, "rainbow, rainbow, rainbow"—the beauty of respect, even awe, for another species.

It is important to note that these first two elements, personification and plot, are connected. In *The Nature of Narrative*, Robert Scholes and Robert Kellogg point out that the eighteenth-century novels of Laurence Sterne demonstrate a way that character *becomes* plot—in other words, the initial situation and sequence leading to a change can be an "internal" one, a shift in the character's thinking.[4] We can see that this psychological focus, already present in the eighteenth-century novels of Sterne, became popular in twentieth-century novels. When we turn to contemporary poetry, we see that same psychological focus. Thus, although we use the term "lyric" for poems in which nothing changes (in which the speaker is repeating the same emotion or observation down the lines), we find that even a lyric can signal change—even a lyric can shift into narrative mode. In Elizabeth Bishop's villanelle "One Art," for example, the speaker keeps losing bigger and bigger things, until in the last stanza she announces that she has lost the person who meant the most to her.

Patterning—the third element of narrative—involves repetition. Patterning can be linguistic or thematic, involving figurative language, an image system, rhetorical devices, formal elements, or rhythm. In "The Fish," we find much that is repeated, including phrases such as "He hadn't fought, he hadn't fought at all" and "I stared . . ." The many metaphors, for instance those comparing the skin of the fish to wallpaper, create another coherence that makes the narrative seem complete.

Armed now with a definition of narrative, we can look carefully and discover narrative in a wide variety of poems. And the first thing we might note is that, even though the word "storytelling" calls to mind the epic and the ballad, poems need not be of *epic* length to tell stories. In other words, narrative can be found in poems that are very short. For example, this little poem by Barbara Guest is just three lines:

*June*

dust dust dust dust dust dust dust
only small rain small rain small
thin thin rain starved rain rin[5]

Observing the June weather, the protagonist/speaker wants rain but gets dust. Her *antagonist* might be said to be the weather. The *initial situation* is "dust," the *sequence of events leading to a change* is "small rain," and the *revelation* made possible by the change is "starved rain rin." Finally, the *pattern* is in the repetition of "dust," "small," "rain," "thin." In such a short poem, the words that are not included in the pattern of repetition—"starved," and "rin"—stand out. Of course this poem also qualifies as a lyric—a song of dust and small rain—but because of the change from *dust* to *rain* to *rin*, its narrative dimension is actually stronger than its lyric dimension.

Not one of these three elements of narrative—personification, plot, and patterning—necessarily takes up much space, but recognizing them leads to an understanding of how a poem works and what it means. Moreover, recognizing the missing or weaker elements of narrative in poems, as Brian McHale argues, also helps us read them.[6]

In the twentieth century, we find that nearly every major

theorist has treated narrative, including formalists and structuralists, feminists, Marxists, rhetoricians, psychoanalysts, reader-response theorists, and historians. But for the last two hundred years until very recently (with the burgeoning of creative nonfiction), the genre of the novel was the most widely read container for narrative, and thus it became the center of critical attention to narrative. That critical attention is a valuable dimension to the close reading of poems.

What do contemporary poets have to say about narrative? In an essay on the temperaments of poetry, Gregory Orr opposes narrative and lyric as "impulses" that "limit" each other.[7] Heather McHugh believes that lyric aspects "unsettle" and "undermine the constitutional groundwork of narration."[8] Meanwhile critics have contributed to the binary opposition between lyric and narrative, taking part in what Heather Dubrow calls a "game" and demonstrating "a covert need on the part of authors and critics to celebrate one form as lacking the limitations and dangers of another."[9] But my concern here is not the game presently taking place between *critics* of lyric and *critics* of narrative. My concern here is the way narrative has created an erroneous divide among poets for the last thirty years.

Interestingly, narrative has been championed by socially conservative poets who also favor the use of rhyme and meter. But narrative has been largely ignored—and even maligned—by poets who see language as ideological and wish to challenge existing ideology. Both groups, however, have misused the term "narrative" and/or confused it with ancillary effects such as realism. And so, while two poetic camps seemed to have formed through this use and misuse of the term "narrative," the argument can be made that the line between narrative and nonnarrative poems is not as distinct as many seem to think.

At the outset, it is important to keep in mind that even though many poems do not upon first glance seem like "narrative poems," they actually do tell or imply stories. It is also important to keep in mind that the presence of a narrative element does not signify any political view except insofar as it implies we live in a world in which we can make sense of experience in time. Narrative, as Roland Barthes points out, "is present in every age, in every place, in every society; it begins with the very history of mankind and there nowhere is nor has been a people without narrative."[10] Cognitive literary theorist Mark Turner goes so far as to argue that narrative organizes not just memory but the whole of human experience, life as it is lived. To oversimplify narrative in poems, then, does a disservice to it and to poetry.[11]

What then of the dissatisfaction with narrative represented by such theorists as Frederic Jameson,[12] François Lyotard,[13] Michel de Certeau,[14] Catherine Belsey,[15] and many postmodern poet-critics such as Charles Bernstein?[16] It seems to stem from two assumptions: first that narrative creates a unified, stable subject position, and second that plots reinforce ideology, thereby preventing social change.

In the first instance, critics focus on personification—the making of characters who are recognizable because they are coherent, predictable, and knowable. Indeed, we know that much of the pleasure in realist novels stems from these stable elements: we "get to know" the characters, become involved in plots, anticipating the "click" of a satisfying ending, whether happy or sad. Readers create characters from signs, and this happens in poems as it does in other kinds of literature. Readers of poems try to make sense, and thus read character into art, for instance by assuming a speaker for a poem. But we know that real human beings are neither as knowable nor as predictable as literary characters.

In the second instance—plot—critics have focused on its element of closure. Paul Ricoeur notes that until the story is finished, the identity of each character or person remains open to revision.[17] "If only the plot would leave people alone," writes poet Bob Perelman in "Anti-Oedipus,"[18] suggesting the irresistible force of ideology. Poet-critic Susan Stewart is also troubled by narrative's insistence on teleology and closure.[19]

Beyond these problems with closure, contemporary dissatisfaction with narrative also stems from the idea that plots reinforce ideology and prevent social change. Jerome McGann believes that for postmodern poets, "narrativity is an especially problematic form of discourse . . . because its structures lay down 'stories' which serve to limit and order the field of experience, in particular the field of social and historical experience." Narrative is "a form of continuity," he says, and as such it is "a way of legitimizing established forms of social order, as well as the very idea of such established forms."[20] In other words narrative is "an inherently conservative" feature of discourse. Theorist Jean-François Lyotard declares that narrative is "the quintessential form of customary knowledge."[21] The problem with narrativity, it seems, is its very *continuity* with its experience.

We know that the web of assumptions a culture deems normal can be so embedded in the social fabric that change is not only hard but also extremely slow in coming. A culture that assumes the dominance of the white race considers white skin the default and dark skin noteworthy; a culture that assumes male dominance considers the male pronoun the default. Just as the plot and the characters in a novel *reveal* the norms of a particular culture, they also *reinforce* those norms, which are by definition constricting. For example, one might say that the novels of Jane Austen underscore patriarchy and heterosexual marriage, while the novels of Terry McMillan underscore capitalism.

We can readily see these two "problems" with narrative—character and plot—in the realism of nineteenth-century novels, such as those by Charles Dickens and George Eliot, wherein apparently omniscient and stable narrators present their plots ending in marriage or death. In general, most novels do construct people (character) as subjects. The alliance of narrative and realism goes back to Aristotle's belief that narrative requires the imitation of action. But if we understand narrative as a *structure*, Roland Barthes argues, then realism is not a motivator of narrative, and narrative does not itself imitate.[22] If we return to our analysis of Barbara Guest's "June" for a moment, we see that structure (narrative) can be separated from the genre (poetry) that contains it.

Moreover, even the most apparently conservative nineteenth-century novels contain features that undermine stability, and almost every novel can also be read as a critique of its characters, ideals, and closure. Repeated plots and archetypal characters are a way a society speaks to itself, as Phillipe Sollers said about the novel, and that speech is not a simple monologue.[23] Loose ends, inconsistencies, and contradictions encourage subversive (or deconstructive) readings.

The predictable elements and hidden codes of fiction led

postmodern fiction writers such as John Barth, John Fowles, and Kathy Acker to work against them, producing narratives without omniscience, coherent characters, plausible plots, or closure. For instance, at the end of Barth's *The Sot-weed Factor*, the narrator neither confirms nor denies the reincarnation of a central character, coyly allowing readers to believe what they wish.[24] Referring to postmodern play with character, Roland Barthes points out that "if a portion of contemporary literature radically interferes with the 'character,' it is not in order to destroy it (which is not possible) but to depersonalize it (which is quite different)."[25] He refers to Phillipe Sollers' novel *Drame*, but I might add Paul Auster's detective novel *Ghosts* as a novel that depersonalizes its characters.

A parallel trend in poems is what Jerome McGann calls "antinarrative," citing Byron's *Don Juan* and Blake's *Milton* as examples of "problematic, ironical, and fundamentally . . . satiric" dialectic poems. In other words, some poems critique narrative within their structures. By contrast, McGann names "nonnarratives" such as Blake's *The Marriage of Heaven and Hell*, which "do not issue calls for change and alterity; they embody in themselves some form of cultural difference."[26] *The Marriage of Heaven and Hell* is nonnarrative in part because "the verbal discourse evolves as a set of images, decorations, and pictures." Whereas antinarratives make ironic use of narrative, nonnarratives try to disregard it entirely.

Thus, while *not* telling stories is a form of narrative critique, telling them *with a wink* is also a critique. And whether the critique comes in the form of the author's conscious or unconscious undermining of narrative elements or in the reader's questioning, narrative is not by itself "conservative" or "radical." Disgruntlement with narrative can be another way of expressing disgruntlement with ideology and the status quo. In other words, if we want to change the world but cannot (or don't want to) avoid stories, then changing the stories we tell and the way we tell them is a place to start.

Robert von Hallberg introduces different oppositional terms: "accommodative versus oppositional." And then we have Charles Bernstein's "absorptive versus antiabsorptive." Bernstein points out that poems of absorption do not call attention to their artifice and thus allow readers to concentrate on content, while anti-absorptive poems remind the reader of the ideological norms of grammar, plot, and character by subverting these norms and drawing attention to their status as made objects. In his poem "What," Ron Silliman argues that radical poems reject the master narratives of ideology. It is interesting that Bernstein praises Silliman's own poems for working against "the deep slumber of chronology, causality, and false unity (totalization)."[27]

But once again a tendency toward binary opposition misleads. Theory shows us that even the most "absorptive" poems can be read against the grain and exposed as made objects. Furthermore, as early as 1966 Roland Barthes noted the tendency of bourgeois society and mass culture itself to de-emphasize narrative coding, pointing out that bourgeois realism "insists on having signs that do not look like signs," while "only 'avant garde' literature still dreams of providing protocols."[28] Ultimately, the binary opposition of "absorptive" and "nonabsorptive" is misleading because we know that readers can create characters and plots out of the thinnest materials. Readers of poetry are forever assuming a coherent speaker (*character*) for a poem, for example, and are also forever alert to the smallest *change* in situation. Conversely, even the most apparently conservative or "absorptive" texts contain features that undermine stability, and can also be read as a critique of their characters, ideals, and closure. Deconstruction has taught us that even narratives that initially seem perfectly constructed and noncontradictory are subject to slippage and non-sense when the reader stops ignoring the bits that don't fit. Similarly, poems that might (when quickly read) seem easily understood and tightly constructed can fall apart in a close reader's hands, as any workshop participant has experienced.

Philip Levine is known as a narrative poet, and his poem "Photography 2" has as its subject an art allied with realism:

*Photography 2*

Across the road from Ford's a Mrs. Strempek
planted tulip bulbs and irises even though
the remnants of winter were still hanging on

in grey speckled mounds. Smoking at all times,
she would kneel, bare legged, on the hard ground
and smile when I passed coming or going
as she worked her trowel back and forth for hours
making a stubborn little hole and when that
was done making another.
                              When Charles Sheeler
came to Dearborn to take his famous photographs
of the great Rouge plant he caught some workers,
tiny little men, at a distance, dwarfed
under the weight of the tools they thought
they commanded. When they got too close,
he left them out of focus, gray lumps with white
wild eyes. Mainly he was interested in
the way space got divided or how light
changed nothing.
                              Nowhere does Mrs. Strempek
show up in all the records of that year,
nor do the few pale tulips and irises
that bloomed in the yard of her rented house
long gone to fire. For the first time I was
in love that spring and would walk the long mile
from the bus stop knowing it was useless,
at my feet the rutted tracks the trucks made,
still half frozen. Ahead the slag heaps
burning at all hours, and the great stacks
blackening the sky, and nothing in between.[29]

The speaker remembers the spring of his "useless" first love
against a background of Sheeler's industrial photographs and a
description of a working-class woman in her yard. The speaker
wants us to believe in the veracity of his "word photograph," ver-
sus Sheeler's deceptive camera photographs; Sheeler is only in-
terested in light and shadow, whereas the speaker is committed
to the human element, of his (undescribed) love and a woman
gardener he remembers. The speaker wants to believe in love
but reality does not let him, just as the industrial setting looms
large over (and eventually erases) the promise of flowers.

Read more closely, however, the poem is full of discrepancies,
mistakes, and contradictions. For example, tulip bulbs are plant-
ed in November, not in March. Irises from rhizomes (rather

than bulbs) are planted in spring, but they do not require deep holes. There are no bulbs that would be planted in late winter in Michigan. Moreover, if the house is small, how large could the yard be? The first stanza suggests that the speaker passed Mrs. Strempek planting bulbs on more than one occasion and that the work took many hours on several days. This underscores the theme of hard work but is mimetically problematic. The last stanza describes "a few pale tulips or irises": is the speaker suggesting that Mrs. Strempek planted hundreds of bulbs, but only a few actually bloomed? The speaker might have thought he was seeing Mrs. Strempek plant tulip bulbs, or he is making up Mrs. Strempek altogether, creating a fictional character and a situation against a canvas of "unreal" photographs. He hints at the possibility of a fiction: "Nowhere does Mrs. Strempek show up in all the records of that year." Although the apparent meaning of this sentence is that Mrs. Strempek was not artful enough a subject for a photographer (though she merits the speaker's linguistic and realistic description), it can also be read as a revelation that the speaker has made up both character and situation. Thus the poem undermines its own premises, making the reader more prone to believe Sheeler's obvious artifice than the speaker's artlessness.

The last line provides another contradiction: the speaker sees "nothing in between" the slag heaps and the stacks. The "nothing" might be read as a trope for the hopelessness of working in industry, but both the first and third stanzas describe Mrs. Strempek planting and the speaker's walk from the bus stop. "In between" are Sheeler's photographs. Thus the poem again undermines its theme of privileging one art form over another. Which is more real—the artful industrial photograph or the artless human reminiscence? Finally, the gap the poem alludes to, but fails to integrate into its description, is the connection between the speaker's hopeless first love and Mrs. Strempek's hopeful act of planting. If the speaker-protagonist wants to use memory to make an art more faithful than photography, his antagonist is his own unreliable memory. The *initial situation* is the picture of Mrs. Strempek planting bulbs, and *the sequence leading to a reversal* of the situation is the fact that Mrs. Strempek does not "show up" in records, and the picture is seen as a figment of the imagination. Read this way, the *revelation* made possible is that all art—including out-of-focus photographs and out-of-focus stories—manipulates reality.

Brian McHale argues that avant-garde narrative poets—John Ashbery, Lyn Hejinian, Michael Palmer, Leslie Scalapino, and Kathleen Fraser—"evoke narrative forms of coherence without ever fully submitting to them."[30] But perhaps it is impossible for *any* poem to "fully submit" to a narrative form of coherence, as I have tried to show in my reading of Philip Levine's "Photography 2." A reader creates coherence or incoherence through what she does or does not see.

In contrast to the plainspoken, "natural," and realist work of a poet like Philip Levine, we have the work of John Ashbery, whose Pulitzer Prize–winning *Self-Portrait in a Convex Mirror* functioned as a manifesto for postmodern poetry when it was published in 1975. The title poem of that book argues for a reassessment of realism. But just as in the era of the Italian painter Parmigianino mannerism replaced realism, the very self-consciousness that Ashbery advocated—and practiced so fluently—is now commonplace among poets. Thus contemporary poetry in the United States has developed its own version of mannerism.

John Ashbery's "Forties Flick" takes for its subject another realistic genre: film, specifically film noir of the 1940s. Whereas Levine's "Photography 2" features a first-person speaker whose coherence, upon examination, is questionable, the speaker of "Forties Flick" is coherent despite the lack of the pronoun "I." In other words, "Photography 2" only pretends to uphold narrative realism, while "Forties Flick" obviously critiques it.

*Forties Flick*

The shadow of the Venetian blind on the painted wall
Shadows of the snake plant and cacti, the plaster animals
Focus the tragic melancholic of the bright stare
Into nowhere, a hole like the black holes in space.
In bra and panties she sidles up to the window:
Zip! Up with the blind. A fragile street scene offers itself,
With wafer thin pedestrians who know where they are going.
The blind comes down slowly, the slats are slowly tilted up.

Why must it always end this way?
A dais with the woman reading, with the ruckus of her hair
And all that is unsaid about her pulling us back to her, with
  her
Into the silence that night alone can't explain.
Silence of the library, of the telephone with its pad,
But we didn't have to reinvent those either:
They had gone away into the plot of the story,
The "art" part—knowing what important details to leave out
And the way character is developed. Things too real
To be of much concern, hence artificial, yet now all over the
  page,
The indoors with the outside becoming part of you
As you find you never left off laughing at death,
The background, dark vine at the edge of the porch.[31]

The poem's dominant mode is description, as the title sig-
nals. The first stanza begins with scene setting, a common fea-
ture of film noir, in this case a scene that features a woman in
"bra and panties," her state of undress a parallel to the seduction
offered by the rest of the setting. The shadows of the artifacts in
the scene suggest the reverberating effect of image. Things cast
shadows in film in the same way that words represent things: par-
tially, open to interpretation, mysteriously. The Venetian blind
functions as a trope for the partial views of the characters in the
film, the watchers of the film, and the readers of the poem. The
blind is both manipulated and manipulative—first in its condi-
tion as "slats" and then by being raised and lowered. The blind
cuts into a secondary scene or prevents it from being seen at all.
Similarly, the film itself manipulates viewers.

The second stanza questions character formation in art: film
noir characters are created through light and darkness—in this
particular case through "all that is unsaid about her" as well as
through what *is* said about her. The silence—what is not said—is
paralleled to what is not shown, what is left out. "The art part"
is that of selection that is dictated by conventions of the genre.
Real versus artificial, inside versus outside, light versus darkness,
said versus unsaid—these are some of the binary oppositions the
poem questions. What is "all over the page"—like blood—is *lan-*

*guage.* Camera technique is a parallel to poet's selection of details; both necessitate "things too real," resulting in a work of art.

The "background, dark vine" of death in "Forties Flick" is not only the plot of film noir. The background of death might be said to apply to every work of art with time and human mortality cast as its shadow. It is a truism that the two eternal subjects for poetry are love and death, and that those two are often combined. "Why must it always end this way" is Ashbery's questioning of plot—and mortality. Here the "forties flick" becomes an emblem of mannerism, which unlike realism does not allow us to forget its status as art, but rather calls attention to it, the manipulative part of the charm. Ashbery's poem, critiquing its own devices, is postmodern. Although its dominant mode is description, one can also read it as a narrative: the speaker is the protagonist who wants the film (or life) to end differently, differently than the genre's convention. Thus the speaker's antagonist can be seen as the genre itself.

On the other side of the debate about narrative are the (mostly) social conservatives, who see culture in the United States as declining, and wish therefore to restore earlier values. In brief, they argue that it wasn't until the current wave of "inaccessible" poetry (such as Ashbery's) written for an audience of (usually academic) peers, that poets in the United States stopped writing narrative for a "general audience." As Stephen Yenser and Marjorie Perloff have shown, this argument both ignores earlier "inaccessible" poetry and misrepresents the audience for poetry.[32] Yet the argument appears with regularity and prominence, notably in poet-critic Dana Gioia's *Can Poetry Matter?*

> Although superficially unrelated to the use of rhyme and meter, the revival of narrative verse allowed the young writers to address several of the broad cultural problems that initially led them back to formal poetry. First, it gave them an inclusive literary mode that, however out of favor with academic theorists, nonetheless has immediate appeal to the non-specialist reader of novels and short stories. Second, narrative provided young poets with a genre that avoided the excessive narcissism of the confessional style (which had often vitiated the work of the older generation) and yet allowed them to write directly

about highly emotional situations. Third, it gave them the opportunity for innovation because narrative poetry has not been actively explored by American writers since the days of Frost and Jeffers. Finally—and most subtly—narrative poetry helped fill the void left by the diminishment of the common cultural context. A story, by definition, creates its own context as it progresses. The self-contained psychological, social and cultural contexts that fiction constructs in the reader's mind allow the narrative to tighten at certain moments and achieve powerfully lyric moments—"epiphanies," as a Joycean might call them—that represent the quintessential poetic effect.[33]

While it is not true that poets tend to write less narrative, and neither is it true that academics have neglected *narrative* verse as opposed to lyric, it *is* true that fewer scholars have studied poetry since the 1970s, primarily because fiction and nonfiction provide a more easily identifiable cultural context, and because that context lends itself to culturally based criticism. Moreover, fiction and nonfiction tend toward the metonymic pole, as David Lodge has shown, one that anchors the work in history, more easily permitting cultural analysis.[34]

It was around 1980 that the two critical camps began forming in the wars over narrative poetry. That was the year Ronald Reagan took office, the end of a decade of intense upheaval in U.S. poetry—upheaval that took the form of challenges to the white male hegemony from women and writers of color. Meanwhile language poets were intent on bridging the rift between literary theory and the practice of poetry. In 1980, in an essay entitled "Reflections on Narrative Poetry," Louis Simpson seems to confuse realism with narrative, noting that novelists consider it their duty to imitate life while poets pride themselves in their removal from it, and that "poetry has been impoverished" because of this trend. He argues that narrative poetry (that which imitates life) energizes poetry, and also makes it accessible.[35]

Such praise of "accessibility" is shared by most pronarrative poets and critics, but in truth it is an issue separate from both narrative and realism. In an era when public attention to—and consumption of—literature is ever shrinking, it would seem that poets who emphasize narrative, realism, and accessibility want to borrow the novel's popularity and related commercial success. Yet poetry's slice of that public attention has always been small.

When proponents of metrical verse found its alliance with narrative in 1981, the new camp was named "expansive poetry" or "new narrative," and was championed by Frederick Feirstein, Frederick Turner, and Dick Allen. According to Allen, expansive poetry uses rhyme, meter, and narrative to make a poetic point. In this way it differs from much of twentieth-century American poetry, which relies on free verse and experimentation for impact. Spurred by what seems a disgruntlement with most twentieth-century poetry, Allen both oversimplifies and misidentifies narrative, at the same time linking it to the use of rhyme and meter. The new narrative group excludes Beat poets, confessional poets, Naked and Open Form and projectivist poets, New Surrealist poets, Language poets, New York school poets, and performance poets.

Similarly, and also in 1981, Mark Jarman and Robert McDowell voiced a plea in *The Reaper* for poems built on a solid foundation of logic and narrative, making themselves clear in "The Reaper's Nonnegotiable Demands": "No more emotion without narrative. Emotion is inconsequential unless it is the result of a story. The story is communal; it is for others. The inconsequential emotion is the one felt only by the poet himself."[36] Mark Jarman provided a checklist for good poems (emphasis in bold is mine):

**A beginning, a middle, an end.**
**Observation.**
**Compression of time.**
Containment.
**Illumination of private gestures.**
Understatement.
Humor.
**Location.**
**Memorable characters.**
A compelling subject.

Jarman and McDowell put together their list as a way of protesting postmodern poetry, the challenge to the coherent self, and

117

the notion of ideology. Note that the items highlighted in bold are attributes shared by realist fiction.

We might read Levine's "Photography 2" again in the light of the demand by Jarman and McDowell for "a beginning, a middle, and an end." Of course, every poem has these elements by virtue of being printed or recited in time and space—in other words, the beginning, middle, and end of every poem (except those in hypertext) are easy to determine by anyone reading or listening to them. I suspect that what Jarman and McDowell are really asking of poems here is an adherence to obvious chronology and/or a narrative arc, an adherence that simplifies almost any *character*-based narrative. In the case of Levine's "Photography 2," does Mrs. Strempek's planting of tulip bulbs constitute the "beginning," and if so, how does that help us read the poem? In fact, the difference between the elements of the plot and order in which they are told is what makes much narrative interesting.

A postmodern poem that critiques narrative is Robert Pinsky's "Poem with Lines in Any Order," a self-consciously out-of-order narrative of a stereotyped working-class family:

> Sonny said, Then he shouldn't have given Molly the two
> more babies.
> Dave's sister and her husband adopted the baby, and that
> was Babe.
> You can't live in the past.
> Sure he was a tough guy but he was no hero.
> Sonny and Toots went to live for a while with the Braegers.
> It was a time when it seemed like everybody had a nickname.
> Nobody can live in the future.
> When Rose died having Babe, Dave came after the doctor
> with a gun.
> Toots said, what do you expect, he was a young man and
> there she was.
> Sonny still a kid himself when Dave moved out on Molly.
> The family gave him Rose's cousin Molly to marry so she
> could raise the children.
> There's no way to just live in the present.
> In their eighties Toots and Sonny still arguing about their
> father.
> Dave living above the bar with Della and half the family.[37]

The stereotype provides us with a false assurance that we understand the story, and meanwhile the poem's very form makes us realize how, as readers, we desire coherent narrative. A reconstruction of the family history might be as follows: Rose and Dave have a third child named Babe, during whose birth Rose dies. Dave's sister adopts Babe, while Dave marries his dead wife's cousin, Molly, but then leaves her and lives with Della while either Molly or the Braegers raise his two other children, Toots and Sonny.

What is the "beginning, middle, and end" of this out-of-order narrative poem? If the *protagonists* are Toots and Sonny, what they *want* is to understand their father's behavior, and their *antagonist*—what keeps them from that understanding—is human nature. The *plot* is harder to unravel. One could say that the *initial situation* is the loss of the mother, and that the *sequence leading to a change* is their being raised by the Braegers and Molly; and the *revelation* made possible by the change is the fact that men like Dave have a hard time being fathers. But the initial situation might also be Dave's emotional state after losing his first wife. Every narrative has to make decisions about what to omit and what to highlight, and chronology is not often the best way to tell a story.

As one might expect in a poem "about" time, Barbara Guest's twenty-four-page poem "The Türler Losses" is a narrative.[38] The speaker recounts the purchase of two Türler watches in Zurich, and parallels their subsequent loss to the loss of a relationship. The speaker wants all three back—the watches, the relationship, the time—but her antagonist is the very irreversibility of time. In modernist fashion, the poem doesn't begin with the purchase of the watches, or with the relationship, but with an ode to a nighthawk and a contemplative collage of memory: "Wrist watches surround themselves with danger," the speaker tells us. After she loses the Türlers, she keeps time with Timex, representing an economic reversal. My point is that Guest's mixed-up chronology does not alter the narrative mode of her poem. Guest was a part of the New York school of poets that included Ashbery, and her status as an avant-garde poet is secure. This is true despite the fact that "The Türler Losses" fulfills every one of Jarman and McDowell's checklist requirements.

While Dana Gioia thinks narrative gives young poets an alternative to narcissism (presumably because they will be telling stories about other people), poet Tony Hoagland thinks that narrative "has been tainted by its over-use in thousands of confessional poems," giving it an "odor of indulgence."[39] Thus the term "narrative" is linked with yet another term, this time "confessional." Of course, while many first-person and apparently autobiographical poems are narratives, so are many other kinds of poems. When Hoagland says he believes that the "narrative form" is more viable and interesting than the "lyric associative fragment," he reveals his complaint to be about "poems of the moment" that are "disassociative," the same complaint as that of Jarman and McDowell. (Who and what determine "over-use" is another issue.) However, narrative in poems is neither altruistic nor narcissistic, and as with every other formal element, *how* it is executed determines its success.

Linda Aldrich's "Enfoldment" is a good poem to look at with respect to narrative and its execution:

*Enfoldment*

The vanilla smell of Ponderosa pine in high summer
is a good thing with visitors: take them up the hill,
pull back a bit of bark, put their noses to it: Ask them
does it smell like chocolate, strawberry, or vanilla?
They make their choices, delighted as children.
Part of having a good time here. Dispelling the fear
they have of communal life. Normalcy at all costs.
Next try the organic vegetable garden, pull a carrot.
The hydroponic greenhouse (emphasize its sterility,
what a good job Carol and team do with that).
Show the baby animals at the farm. Let them hold
a baby goat. Give them some free-range eggs for free.
Tell the story of the chicken frozen in the puddle and
Judy's hair dryer. Show the bull, but only if they have
the right shoes. Show the antique fire engine. Tell stories
of using it to put out neighbors' fires in the valley:
the 7th Day Adventists next door (a subtle comparison):
how they're a little weird, the women in skirts and kerchiefs,
how they go walking on Saturdays, stay away from machines.

At dinner, whatever you do, make sure
your guests sit with people who know how to do it
right: who will not ask too many questions, or laugh
overly at everything, or try to make them come to
service on Wednesday or Saturday or Sunday,
or answer questions too completely. Especially
about Uranda. Of course with his picture on the wall,
they're bound to ask something, but keep it simple.
In general, avoid talking about spiritual issues unless
they show interest over time. No matter what, avoid
talk of sex and relationships. They will not understand.
Point out the married couples with children in the dining
room. The wonderful cross-section of ages. Relate
a homespun anecdote. Louise and her cinnamon roll
parties is a good one. Or how the two-pits-on-top-of-each-
can-of-peaches got started. But don't give out a can of
    peaches.
There weren't enough this year.

For godsakes, keep them away from Norm.
You know how he can be.

And Miriam with her list of ailments.

Show them to the door with a loaf of home-made seed
bread, or a jar of yoghurt. Tell them how much
you enjoyed sharing your home with them.
Be enthusiastic. Firm handshake or hug.
Straightforward eyes. The world is hungry
for spirit and community. They'll probably come back.
If they don't, it's because they don't resonate.
Not the right substance. Let it go.
Remember: Everything finds its own level.[40]

"Enfoldment" takes place in the context of a spiritual communi-
ty, more specifically the Emissaries of Divine Light, a spiritual or-
ganization founded in 1932 by Lloyd Arthur Meeker (who took
the alias Uranda). The group's stated purpose is to "encourage
the experience and expression of divine identity." The speaker
is showing a newer convert how to give tours of the community,

highlighting its good points and avoiding those areas (notably sex and the members' attachment to Uranda) that might raise suspicion. The poem's dominant mode is argument (act this way when giving tours), but when we apply a narrative framework, we see other interesting aspects. In a sense, the speaker wants the listener to "buy" his or her script, so that the *antagonist* is actually the listener, who must hear the script with all its embedded contradictory messages. And we, the readers, are the *witnesses* who learn. We learn the hypocrisies of the community through the salesmanship of the speaker, who brings up, for instance, the Seventh-Day Adventists, and their "odd" practices while trying to hide his own community's even odder practices.

The *initial situation* might be termed the reader's willingness to be charmed, *the sequence leading to a change* is the unraveling of how the community works (dispelling the charm), and the *revelation* made possible by this change is the insight that this community puts its best foot forward and hides skeletons in its closets, along with the larger insight that every dramatic monologue is a pointed rhetorical act. The bolded words and phrases contribute dramatic irony in the same way that the admonition for "straightforward eyes" suggests exactly the opposite of straightforwardness. Interestingly, the stories mentioned in the poem (chicken and hair dryer, antique fire engine, peach pits, etc.) serve to reinforce the propaganda of the rhetoric, suggesting that every narrative is in some way built for a purpose.

Narrative seems to dominate Eleanor Wilner's "The Girl with Bees in Her Hair." The title announces both the characterization (the girl) and the potential plot (bees in one's hair are a problem). Upon analysis, however, the poem is missing a necessary element of narrative, an absence that points to our postmodern condition.

*The Girl with Bees in Her Hair*

came in an envelope with no return address;
she was small, wore a wrinkled dress of figured
cotton, full from neck to ankles, with a button
of bone at the throat, a collar of torn lace.
she was standing before a monumental house—
on the scale you see in certain English films:

urns, curved drives, stone lions, and an entrance far
too vast for any home. She was not of that place,
for she had a foreign look, and tangled black hair,
and an ikon, heavy and strange, dangling from
an oversize chain around her neck, that looked
as if some tall adult had taken it from his,
and hung it there as a charm to keep her safe
from a world of infinite harm that soon
would take him far from her, and leave her
standing, as she stood now—barefoot, gazing
without expression into distance, away
from the grandeur of that house, its gravel
walks and sculpted gardens. She carried a basket
full of flames, but whether fire or flowers
with crimson petals shading toward a central gold,
was hard to say—though certainly, it burned,
and the light within it had nowhere else
to go, and so fed on itself, intensified its red
and burning glow, the only color in the scene.
the rest was done in grays, light and shadow
as they played along her dress, across her face,
and through her midnight hair, lively with bees.
At first they seemed just errant bits of shade,
until the humming grew too loud to be denied
as the bees flew in and out, as if choreographed
in a country dance between fields of sun
and the black tangle of her hair.
                              Without warning
a window on one of the upper floors flew open—
wind had caught the casement, a silken length
of curtain filled like a billowing sail—the bees
began to stream out of her hair, straight
to the single opening in the high façade. Inside,
a moment later—the sound of screams.

The girl—who had through all of this seemed
unconcerned and blank—all at once looked up.
She shook her head, her mane of hair freed
of its burden of bees, and walked away,
out of the picture frame, far beyond
the confines of the envelope that brought her
image here—here, where the days grow longer

now, the air begins to warm, dread grows to
fear among us, and the bees swarm.[41]

This poem has all the surface aspects of narrative, including an
omniscient narrator, yet is missing a clear protagonist and an-
tagonist. Unlike a fairy tale or nineteenth-century realism, it's
hard to tell who wants something in this poem. But the poem's
real shortcoming as narrative is most significant in determining
how it works. The only hint that the narrator is at all involved in
the story is at the end: "dread grows to fear among us." That is
also where the poem changes from past tense to present, with
the word "here." The "girl with bees in her hair" seems to want
something because she is approaching the great house, yet she
is not particularly disturbed by the bees in her hair, so we can't
really say she wants to get rid of the bees even though they are
termed a "burden" at the end of the poem. The inhabitants of
the house "scream" when the bees enter, so presumably they
want to get rid of the bees. The bees themselves provide the most
interesting aspect of desire: they leave the girl's hair and enter
the house. The bees swarm. In other words, *the human characters
in the poem seem to have no desires except reactive ones, while the bees
have agency.* What does it mean when bees and not humans have
agency? Perhaps the humans in this world have been so shaped
by ideology that they can no longer even "want" or "not want"—
they are helpless in the face of "foreign" influence or intrusion.

If the *initial situation* of the poem is the arrival of a "for-
eign" child carrying danger but somehow protected from it,
the *sequence leading to a change* is the bees streaming into the
house, and the *revelation* made possible by the change is the
"dread changing to fear." Both "dread" and "fear" are Anglo-
Saxon "gut" words, very similar in meaning. One connotation
of "dread," however, is the "dreadlock," the twisted strands of
kinky hair when it grows long, and an image of black hair that
recalls Toni Morrison's character Beloved in the novel of the
same name. If the foreign child is a black child, the poem can
be read as pointing to race relations in the United States, with
the black outsider carrying swarms of bees that terrify the white
inhabitants.

A poem that mixes modes, and thus subverts narrative, is Lucie Brock-Broido's "Self Deliverance by Lion," in which a plot is suggested in the title, but the first four lines proceed as argument:

*Self-Deliverance by Lion*

To maul is to make a massive loss
Of the history of a body's history.

What will be taken will be the custody
Of soft tissue, and astonishment.

Her hair was a long damp chestnut
River-pelt spilled after an enormous

And important rain. Her body was still sticky
With the lilac repetitions in her cotton dress.

She was found face-up on a cold March morning
By the most menial and tender of the keepers

At the zoo, crewelled with frost marks, redolent
As the retractile dewclaws on a lion's forepaw, massive

And significant. I had hoped for, all that Serengeti
Year, a hopelessness of less despair

Than hope itself. The excellent repair
Of night fell cruel and quickly where

The lions had the mastery of me—aware
Their mastery was by my will, and fair.[42]

This poem has the dominant mode of argument: To die is also to lose a body's history. Whether the body is embalmed or cremated, what makes it distinctive as a body is lost, transformed by formaldehyde or burned into ash. But we can also read the poem as a narrative, the *protagonist* being the woman at the zoo who commits suicide by climbing into the lion's den, who wants hope in the form of release (i.e., death) from painful life. If she gets what she wants, as is suggested in the title, then there is no narrative tension.

The last seven lines of the poem, however, introduce an "I" whose identity is blended with the woman at the zoo. This speaker, unlike the woman at the zoo, is not yet dead. The link between the two is the image of the "dewclaws on a lion's forepaw" and the adjectives, "massive and significant," which apply to the speaker's year rather than the woman in the zoo. Her despair—the trope of the lions—"masters" her because she allows it. Like the woman who climbs over the zoo wall, the speaker offers herself to despair. The last five lines of the poem release her from this condition by emphasizing the lyric through exact end rhymes, the progression of which reveals another narrative in the pattern of "despair," "repair," "where," "aware," "fair." The word "hopelessness" turns to the word "hope." Note the twisting in the last lines—the "excellent repair" that falls "cruelly" and the unanswered question of who is dominant, woman or lions—a twisting that contradicts an optimistic ending and points to chronology as the real ending. Although the "Serengeti Year" is over, the speaker cannot or refuses to make sense of it by resolving it one way or another.

James Galvin's *X*, a book containing a wide range of effects infused with immense energy, begins with "Little Dantesque," a poem that signals its narrative mode from the first line:

*Little Dantesque*

It turns out
The dogs were in control all along.

Hard by the hinges of Hell—

Faculty party.

Everyone drifts
In their disastrous bodies.

Sudden furniture,
A hint of eucalyptus.

Someone plugs in the flowers.

1
I've been a has-been.
Now I'm a was. I was
Promoted.

2
The dogs were in control all along.
They saw everything.

3
I had a happy medium—
Had her reading out of my palm.
The circus folded up and left.
A riot of life-forms
And annoying colors whisked
Like bright scarves up a sleeve.

4
The dogs want out.
How like them.[43]

One can read the poem as the story of someone whose life has "gone to the dogs," with the dogs as variations of Cerberus, the guard dog of Hades. In fact, the title cues us into the fact that the speaker is offering a tour of hell, albeit a little one: he's ironic or modest. His hell is not Dante's communal one, but a personal one. One friend who read an early version of this essay noted that I would be in "bad faith" with the reader if I didn't admit that I was reading the poem as Galvin's autobiography, referencing his divorce from Jorie Graham. My last essay deals more specifically with the case of reading first-person poems as autobiography, but for the moment, I'll admit this aspect and let other readers decide whether it matters. "Little Dantesque" begins with the ending: "It turns out / the dogs were in control all along." Like a modernist narrative whose suspense doesn't rely on *what* happens so much as *how* it happens, the poem tells us in the first line that this story ends badly. Obviously, the narrator is omniscient about the events of the story.

If the speaker is the protagonist, what does he want? In a sense he wants what he has lost, the happy medium, but in another sense, there's nothing that he wants since he can't have what he has lost, and that realization makes the poem tragic. The only beings in the poem who want something are the dogs—and what they want is "out." Like Wilner's "The Girl with Bees in Her Hair," Galvin's "Little Dantesque" undermines the sense of human agency, one of the traditional elements of narrative. If human beings don't want something, their stories lack tension. Similarly, if we know the story will end badly, our goal in reading shifts from "what happened" to "how did it happen."

The tone of "Little Dantesque" is sad because of the disconnected and clipped observations. It is as if the speaker cannot allow himself to elaborate. His life has been so constrained that he has energy only to make these short statements, interrupted by much time, silence, and white space. The bitterness of comparing a "faculty party" to the "hinges of hell" is analogous to the depression inherent in seeing everyone "drift" in "disastrous" bodies. The speaker is wearing dark glasses because the circus—and all its life and color—has departed from his life. The "sudden furniture" and the fact that someone "plugs in the flowers" suggest the mechanization of life, its artificial sources. The speaker is as disconnected from the source of his personhood as from his desires.

As we have noted, the first lines of this poem ("It turns out / The dogs were in control all along") give the ending away, suggesting that the speaker cannot envision a different outcome. Like a story that begins with the ending and then uses flashback to tell the interim events ("had her reading out of my palm," "the circus folded up and left") the poem's structure is not chronological. Note the tangle talk of "had her reading out of my palm" which is a turn of the phrase "eating out of my hand," a pun on palm reading. Reading is more important than eating to this speaker and the departed beloved. But the long vowel rhymes of "all along" and "palm" sound dirge-like, and the future read here is dismal.

The poem's wit ("I've been a has-been. / Now I'm a was. / I was promoted") deserves unpacking. In the past the speaker was a "has-been," which suggests that the best or highest point of his life was in the past, and so he is living on past glory. The departure of the "circus," however, has made him a "was"—not an idiomatic expression in English, but something that suggests that he is no longer alive. We use present tense to talk about people who are "has-beens" because they are still alive; we use "was," the past tense of "is," to refer to someone who is dead. The bitter irony of the speaker considering this "a promotion" makes us ask, promoted to what? Promoted to a deeper circle of hell, perhaps, a darker depression.

The last stanza is deadpan in its irony. Not only has the speaker's life "gone to the dogs," but the dogs "want out," leaving the speaker alone in a void. The overlap of colloquial expressions that refer to quotidian events—pet dogs like to go outside—with the poem as statement of the speaker's life makes its clipped expression especially poignant. Each word costs the speaker something. The short, end-stopped lines allow no continuity of stanza or subject. Beginning each line with a new thought signals the effort involved in speaking at all. Contradicting Ezra Pound's dictum against end-stopping lines and beginning new ones with a "heave," Galvin imbues his poem with the sense of effort. The implied narrative holds together a disjunctive and cryptic poem, and the poem's mixed-up chronology accentuates the tone of dislocation. Galvin is not a poet the pronarrative camp would embrace. Nevertheless, narrative figures strongly in this collection.

We have seen that the term "narrative" is consistently misused, both by U.S. poets who are "for" narrative and those who are against it. Moreover, the term has been confused with effects such as realism and accessibility. Oddly, at the same time that "narrative" has taken on these false associations, postmodern poets like Ed Dorn and Lyn Hejinian have produced vibrant narrative poems, *and* critics like Heather Dubrow, Susan Friedman, Brian McHale, and Marjorie Perloff have illuminated the role of narrative in postmodern poetry. The reason for this disparity rests in yet another binary opposition: that between poets and critics.

Contemporary poets read mostly poetry within their own

camp. Moreover, many poets do not read literary scholarship, and their own attempts at criticism suffer for it. Though U.S. poetry is arguably more lively than it was thirty years ago, with many more poets writing and more books published, poetry criticism *by* poets has lost credibility since the days of Randall Jarrell, due in part, perhaps, to the difficulty in keeping up with an ever-burgeoning field. In thinking about narrative, contemporary poets might consider the dictum of D. H. Lawrence: "Trust the tale, not the teller." Lawrence was discounting the role of biography, and emphasizing the texts themselves. In the same way, contemporary poems themselves tell us the truth about narrative: that it has value as an enduring structure, and that analysis of narrative can yield valuable insights. The poems themselves employ narrative in infinitely more sophisticated and interesting ways than the poets' own criticism would suggest.

As for readers of poetry, they need to be aware that "narrative" in contemporary poems is more common than some say it is. The term "narrative" has become the site of a battlefield for literary readership, with narrative poetry camp calling for "accessible" poetry—which is related to its commercial value. And yet even this value is relative. Best-selling poet Billy Collins is one of a few whose books sell 100,000 copies. Conversely, the average print run for a university or small press publisher of poetry is a mere 2,000 copies. And thus we can see the call for narrative in poetry—even with narrative incorrectly defined—as a call for poetry to enter more fully into the ideology of capitalism, as Dana Gioia's own career marketing Jell-O and other foods might suggest. By writing more accessible poems, poets can "reach more people" and they also make more royalties.

But it is not narrative that makes a poem accessible. Rather it is the simplicity of the ideas and language, and more importantly it is the sophistication of the reader. As Stanley Fish has shown, good readers can access anything. They can even make literature out of random words.[44] If narrative is indeed central to human experience, then it follows that the practice of reading each poem with an eye for how it fits (or doesn't fit) a narrative structure will allow us to understand it more deeply—which of course will allow us to understand ourselves.

130

## Notes

1. Gérard Genette, *Narrative Discourse Revisited*, trans. Jane E. Lewin (Ithaca: Cornell University Press), 19.

2. J. Hillis Miller, "Narrative," in *Critical Terms for Literary Study*, ed. Frank Lentricchia and Thomas McLaughlin (Chicago: University of Chicago Press, 1990), 66–79.

3. Elizabeth Bishop, "The Fish," *Poets.org*, August 31, 2012, http://www.poets.org/viewmedia.php/prmMID/22238.

4. Robert Scholes and Robert Kellogg, *The Nature of Narrative* (Oxford: Oxford University Press, 1968), 192.

5. Barbara Guest, "June," in *Collected Poems* (Middletown, CT: Wesleyan University Press, 2008), 164. Reprinted by permission of Wesleyan University Press.

6. Brian McHale, "Weak Narrativity: The Case of Avant-Garde Narrative Poetry," *Narrative* 9, no. 2 (May 2001), 161–67.

7. Gregory Orr, "Four Temperaments and the Forms of Poetry," in *Poets Teaching Poets: Self and the World*, ed. by Gregory Orr and Ellen Bryant Voigt (Ann Arbor: University of Michigan Press, 1996), 254–68.

8. Heather McHugh, "Moving Means, Meaning Moves," in Orr and Voigt, *Poets Teaching Poets*, 208.

9. Heather Dubrow, "The Interplay of Narrative and Lyric: Competition, Cooperation, and the Case of the Anticipatory," *Narrative* 14, no. 3 (October 2006), 254–71.

10. Roland Barthes, "Introduction to the Structural Analysis of Narratives," in *Image–Music–Text*, trans. Stephen Heath (New York: Hill and Wang, 1977), 79.

11. Mark Turner, *The Literary Mind: The Origins of Thought and Language* (New York: Oxford University Press, 1998).

12. Fredric Jameson, *The Political Unconscious: Narrative as a Socially Symbolic Act* (Ithaca: Cornell University Press, 1981).

13. Jean-François Lyotard, *The Postmodern Condition: A Report on Knowledge*, trans. Geoff Bennington and Brian Massumi (Minneapolis: University of Minnesota Press, 1984).

14. Michel de Certeau, *The Practice of Everyday Life*, trans. Steven Rendall (Berkeley: University of California Press, 2002).

15. Catherine Belsey, *Critical Practice* (New York: Routledge, 2002).

16. Charles Bernstein, *A Poetics* (Cambridge: Harvard University Press, 1992).

17. Paul Ricoeur, *Time and Narrative*, trans. Kathleen McLaughlin and David Pellauer, 3 vols. (Chicago: University of Chicago Press, 2006).

18. Bob Perelman, "Anti-Oedipus," in *A Poetics*, ed. Charles Bernstein (Cambridge: Harvard University Press, 1992), 33.

19. Susan Stewart, *On Longing: Narratives of the Miniature, the Gigantic, the Souvenir, and the Collection* (Durham, NC: Duke University Press, 1993).

20. Jerome McGann, "Contemporary Poetry, Alternate Routes," *Critical Inquiry* 13, no. 3 (Spring 1987), 624–47.

21. Lyotard, *The Postmodern Condition*, 19.

22. Barthes, *Image–Music–Text*, 257.

23. Philippe Sollers, "The Novel and the Experience of Limits," in *Surfiction: Fiction Now . . . and Tomorrow*, ed. Raymond Federman (Athens, OH: Swallow Press, 1981), 61.

24. John Barth, *The Sot-Weed Factor* (New York: Doubleday, 1960), 805.

25. Barthes, *Image–Music–Text*, 257.

26. McGann, "Contemporary Poetry, Alternate Routes," 630.

27. Charles Bernstein, *Content's Dream: Essays, 1975–1984* (Evanston, IL: Northwestern University Press, 1986), 308.

28. Barthes, *Image–Music–Text*, 257.

29. Philip Levine, *The Mercy: Poems* (New York: Knopf, 1999), 16. Used by permission of Alfred A. Knopf, an imprint of the Knopf Doubleday Publishing Group, a division of Random House LLC. All rights reserved.

30. Brian McHale, "Weak Narrativity: The Case for Avant-Garde Poetry," *Narrative* 9, no. 2 (May 2001): 161–167.

31. John Ashbery, "Forties Flick," in *Self-Portrait in a Convex Mirror* (New York: Penguin, 1976), 5. Used by permission of Viking Penguin, a division of Penguin Group (USA) LLC.

32. Stephen Yenser, "Some Poets' Criticism and the Age," *Southern Review* 30, no. 1 (December 1994); Marjorie Perloff, "Poetry Doesn't Matter: Picketing the Zeitgeist," *American Book Review* 15, no. 5 (December 1993–January 1994).

33. Dana Gioia, *Can Poetry Matter?* (Minneapolis: Graywolf Press, 1992), 254–55.

34. David Lodge, *The Modes of Modern Writing; Metaphor, Metonymy, and the Typology of Modern Literature* (Ithaca: Cornell University Press, 1977).

35. Louis Simpson, "Reflections on Narrative Poetry," in *Claims for Poetry*, ed. Donald Hall (Ann Arbor: University of Michigan Press, 1982), 407–16.

36. Mark Jarman and Robert McDowell, "The Reaper's Nonnegotiable Demands," in *The Reaper* (Ashland, OR: Story Line Press, 1996), 40.

37. Robert Pinsky, "Poem with Lines in Any Order," in *Selected Poems*

(New York: Farrar, Straus and Giroux, 2011). Reprinted by permission of Farrar, Straus, and Giroux, LLC.

38. Barbara Guest, *Collected Poems* (Middletown, CT: Wesleyan University Press, 2008).

39. Tony Hoagland, "Fear of Narrative and the Skittery Poem of Our Moment," *Poetry Foundation*, August 31, 2012, http://www.poetryfoundation.org/poetrymagazine/article/177773.

40. Linda Aldrich, *March & Mad Women* (Cincinnati: Cherry Grove, 2012), 52. Reprinted with permission by the author.

41. Eleanor Wilner, *The Girl with Bees in Her Hair* (Port Townsend, WA: Copper Canyon Press, 2004), 75. Reprinted with the permission of The Permissions Company, Inc., on behalf of Copper Canyon Press, www.coppercanyonpress.org.

42. Lucie Brock-Broido, *Trouble in Mind* (New York: Knopf, 2005), 68. Used by permission of Alfred A. Knopf, an imprint of Knopf Doubleday Publishing Group, a division of Random House LLC. All rights reserved.

43. James Galvin, "Little Dantesque," in *X: Poems* (Port Townsend, WA: Copper Canyon Press, 2003), 3. Reprinted with the permission of The Permissions Company, Inc., on behalf of Copper Canyon Press, www.coppercanyonpress.org.

44. Stanley Fish, *Is There a Text in This Class? The Authority of Interpretive Communities* (Cambridge: Harvard University Press, 1982).

# A Sexy New Animal

## *The DNA of the Prose Poem*

*The Prose Poem as a Beautiful Animal* (by Russell Edson)

He had been writing a prose poem, and had succeeded in mating a giraffe with an elephant. Scientists from all over the world came to see the product: The body looked like an elephant's, but it had the neck of a giraffe with a small elephant's head and a short trunk that wiggled like a wet noodle.

You have created a beautiful new animal, said one of the scientists.

Do you really like it?

Like it? Cried the scientist, I adore it, and would love to have sex with it that I might create another beautiful animal.[1]

Over the last fifty years or so, the prose poem has produced much critical wringing of hands. Michael Riffaterre, for example, calls it "the literary genre with the oxymoron for a name."[2] And yet when we define those terms—that is, when we subdivide the genus and species, as it were—we do manage to make the creature's status clearer. If the genre of poetry mates with the form of prose, then the *prose poem* is not an oxymoron, but a hybrid, like the *verse novel* or the *prose play*. As David Lehman puts it, "As soon as you admit the possibility that verse is an adjunct of poetry and not an indispensible quality, the prose poem ceases to be a contradiction in terms."[3]

And unlike ligers and tigons, who produce defective offspring when bred, the prose poem mutts of literature have good healthy DNA, as evidenced by increasing birthrate. One might even say that the prose poem is a hybrid that actually derives its energy from the collision of opposites, notably those between realism and fantasy, and poem and novel. It is possible to sequence the genome of the prose poem. However, in the spirit of this strange and fecund animal, detours and back alleys proliferate.

## What Is "Poetic" Prose?

While *verse* is literature written in lines, *prose* is writing whose margins are determined by the restrictions of the printing technology. Thus, because prose is not necessarily literature, some critics prefer to call prose poems "unlineated verse." Meanwhile, the category of "poetic prose" is usually applied to literature with syntactical and lexical richness, anaphora, tropes, and word play. Suzanne Bernard distinguishes between two kinds of prose writing: plain, and "oratorical,"[4] taking rhythms from formal speeches and from the Bible. Sir Thomas Malory's 1470 *Morte d'Arthur* (one thousand pages) and Fénelon's 1699 *Telemachus* (three hundred pages) have been called "poetic prose romances," because the mode of romance, along with their narrative structure, dominates our perception of them, but also because of the rich writing.

But perhaps setting apart prose that is lexically, syntactically, and figuratively rich might just be another way of saying "good prose." We don't expect much from a driver's manual, but with imaginative literature, style counts. The degree of complexity, however, varies with the prevailing fashion. In eighteenth-century Germany, Novalis—the pen name for Georg Philipp Friedrich Freiherr (Baron) von Hardenberg (1772–1801)—was prompted by grief over the death of his fiancé to publish "Hymns to the Night," twelve pages that intersperse short poetic prose with lyrics, featuring dense diction and syntax. Here's the first paragraph, in an 1897 translation by George McDonald:

> Before all the wondrous shows of the widespread space around him, what living, sentient thing loves not the all-joyous light—

135

with its colors, its rays and undulations, its gentle omnipres-
ence in the form of the wakening Day? The giant-world of
the unresting constellations inhales it as the innermost soul
of life, and floats dancing in its blue flood—the sparkling,
ever-tranquil stone, the thoughtful, imbibing plant, and the
wild, burning multiform beast inhales it—but more than all,
the lordly stranger with the sense-filled eyes, the swaying walk,
and the sweetly closed, melodious lips. Like a king over earth-
ly nature, it rouses every force to countless transformations,
binds and unbinds innumerable alliances, hangs its heavenly
form around every earthly substance. Its presence alone re-
veals the marvelous splendor of the kingdoms of the world.[5]

Later, Jean-Jacques Rousseau wanted to be a "poet en prose,"
that is, a good stylist. So did Gustav Flaubert. Here is Flaubert on
good prose, in a letter to Louise Colet:

What a bitch of a thing prose is! It is never finished, there is
always something to be done over. However, I think it can be
given the consistency of verse. A good prose sentence should
be like a good line of poetry—unchangeable, just as rhythmic,
just as sonorous.[6]

Still later, Stéphane Mallarmé wrote, "There's no such thing
as prose. There's only the alphabet, and then there are verses,
which are more or less closely knit, more or less diffuse. So long
as there is a straining toward style, there is versification."[7]

"Straining toward style" became a key factor in defining the
prose poem. Ron Silliman in *The New Sentence* argues that in the
prose poem, the sentence is "altered for torque, or increased
polysemy/ambiguity," and that the control of syllogistic move-
ment "keeps the reader's attention at or very close to the level of
language, the sentence level or below."[8] Stephen Fredman says
the prose poem evidences "a fascination with language (through
puns, rhyme, repetition, elision, disjunction, excessive troping,
and subtle foregrounding of diction) that interferes with the
progression of story or idea, while at the same time inviting and
examining the 'prose' realms of fact and reclaiming for poetry
the domain of truth."[9]

In addition to linguistic density, some critics require the
prose poem to be short. Suzanne Bernard is the first of many

who require the prose poem to be less than a page long, partly because she believes it morphs into another genre when longer. Max Jacob's imagistic, surreal, and very short poems in *Dice Cup* (1906, 1917) are cited as an influence by many U.S. prose poem writers. In his preface, Jacob writes, "the prose poem is a jewel" that must "submit to the laws of all art, which are style or will and situation or emotion."[10] A jewel is generally small because of its high value; Jacob is suggesting that the heightened style cannot be kept up for too long.

Yet there do exist longer prose poems, at least ones deemed that by their makers. For example, Edgar Allen Poe's 1848 *Eureka: A Prose Poem* (59 pages), Count Lautréamont's 1869 *Chants de Maldoror* (240 pages), William Carlos Williams' 1918 *Kora in Hell: Improvisations* (88 pages), and St.-John Perse's 1924 *Anabasis* (36 pages). *Eureka* reads like a philosophical tract, *Kora in Hell* like diary entries, and *Maldoror* like a surrealist epic. I suspect *Kora in Hell* and *Chants de Maldoror* are not classified as novels because of the absence of realism, recognizable characters, or a plot, so that the term "prose poem" is again used to describe literary works that don't easily fall into established categories.

*Anabasis* is a particularly interesting example because some of the lines are right justified and some are broken, often within the same page. Perse uses anaphora, description, figurative language, and sentence fragments. The poem's subject is the narrator's founding of a mythical city in the ancient East, and an exploration of power. In his translator's preface, T. S. Eliot explains his choice of the term "poem":

> I refer to this poem as a poem. . . . Poetry may occur, within a definite limit on one side, at any point along a line of which the formal limits are "verse" and "prose." Without offering any generalized theory about "poetry," "verse" and "prose," I may suggest that a writer, by using, as does Mr. Perse, certain exclusively poetry methods, is sometimes able to write poetry in what is called prose.[11]

Eliot goes on to say that the system of *Anabasis* is one of "stresses and pauses," as evidenced by "punctuation and spacing is that of poetry and not prose." Here is the beginning of Section IV:

> Such is the way of the world and I have nothing but good
>     to say of it.—Foundation of the City. Stone and bronze.
>     Thorn fires at dawn
>     bared these great
>     green stones, and viscid like the bases of temples, of
>         latrines,
> and the mariner at sea whom our smoke reached saw that
>     the earth to the summit had changed its form (great
>     tracts of burnt-over land seen afar and these operation of
>     channeling the living waters on the mountains).[12]

This mythical content, inspired by (but ungrounded in) history, along with its syntactical and lexical richness, description, and tropes, suggest that *Anabasis* is a poem.

Paul Valéry's theory about the difference between poetry and prose, circa the 1930s, is also based on content, on the purposefulness of prose versus the oblique qualities of poetry. He points out that though poetry and prose "use the same words, the same forms, the same tones," there is an essential difference:

> When the man [who is walking] has completed his movement, when he has reached the place, the book, the fruit, the object he desired, this possession immediately annuls his whole act; the effect consumes the cause, the end absorbs the means . . . only the result remains. . . . It is the same with the use of prose . . . language which has expressed my aim . . . vanishes once it has *arrived*. . . . But the poem, on the contrary, does not die for having been of use; it is purposely made to be reborn from its ashes and perpetually to become what it has been.[13]

Gertrude Stein says something similar when she says prose is about verbs and poetry is about nouns: "Poetry is doing nothing but losing refusing and pleasing and betraying and caressing nouns."[14] Prose gets somewhere, but poetry *is* wherever it is. Thus it is that pragmatism and narrative may appear to be paramount in *Paradise Lost*, but ultimately are secondary to the function of the whole as inspired language. Prose poetry, even though it is unlineated, shares this content-based definition. In a sense, the prose poem has become a sort of grab bag, defined as prose that has the *content* of a poem and is not recognizable as another genre: *not* a novel, *not* a lyric verse poem, *not* a play, *not* an essay, *not* a memoir, etc. Indeed, Russell Edson, one of the masters of the contemporary prose poem, said in an interview, "There is too much emphasis on genre vis-à-vis the prose poem. For me the spirit of the prose poem is writing without genre; to go naked only with one's imagination."[15]

Contemporary poet Charles Simic blends elements to define the prose poem:

> The prose poem reads like a narrative but works like a lyric, since it relies on juxtaposition of images and unexpected turns of phrase. An interrupted narrative, it insists that it has to be read over and over again until its words and images radiate their full mystery.[16]

By something that "reads" differently from the way it works, Simic seems to say that reading a block of prose is quicker than reading a poem with its embedded pauses signaled by line and stanza breaks. Simic of course is also referring to the kind of prose poetry he himself writes.

### The Prose Poem and the Novel

Although the Greeks wrote prose fiction, as did the Japanese in the eleventh century, the novel as we know it in English became popular in the sixteenth to eighteenth centuries. The early novel was a hybrid of travel writing, autobiography, and journalism. A world-creating genre with an emphasis on individual and (in England) often middle-class and realistic characters, the novel "rose," according to Ian Watt's famous theory, at the same time as capitalism.[17] Perhaps it is no accident that the prose poem became popular at about the same time. In fact, I think the prose poem actually evolved as a reaction to realism in the novel.

Novels were usually told in past tense, and it is this recounting of events in the past, *as if they really happened*, that creates realism. The prose poem challenges the novel on the basis of realism, tense, and simulation of history. While Margueritte Murphy argues that each prose poem calls forth a particular genre in order to define itself contrary to it,[18] I think that the most deflected genre is the realist novel. St.-John Perse, for example, rejects the metonymic realism of the novel. He writes, "My entire work, which is one of re-creation, has always moved in regions beyond place and time. Allusive and full of recollections as it may be for me in its final form, it seeks to avoid all historical, and like-wise geographical, points of reference."[19] The novel (think of *Robinson Crusoe*) pretends to be history, while the prose poem is liberated from it. As Catherine Belsey and other critics have argued, realism replicates and enforces the status quo.[20] Reading a realist novel can make one think the world is set in stone. On the other hand, the prose poem, with its otherworldly aspects, is in a better position to be subversive. The prose poem might be termed "good for nothing" *except* subversion, satisfying the need of critics and poets like Calvin Bedient for poetry to be a "practice of social alienation."[21]

The prose poem's root in the novel is articulated most precisely by Joris Karl Huysmans' aesthete narrator (Des Esseintes) in the 1884 novel *A Rebours* (*Against the Grain*). He seeks the prose poem for aesthetic pleasure, mentioning its qualities of compression:

> Of all forms of literature that of the prose poem was Des Esseintes' chosen favorite. Handled by an alchemist of genius, it should, according to him, store up in its small compass, like an extract of meat, so to say, the essence of the novel, while suppressing its long, tedious analytical passages and superfluous descriptions. Again and again Des Esseintes had pondered the distracting problem, how to write a novel concentrated in a few sentences, but which should yet contain the cohobated juice of the hundreds of pages always taken up in describing the setting, sketching the characters, gathering together the necessary incidental observations and minor details. In that case, so inevitable and unalterable would be the words selected that they must take the place of all others. . . .
>
> The novel, thus conceived, thus condensed in a page or two, would become a communion, an interchange of thought between a magic-working author and an ideal reader. . . . In a

word, the prose poem represented in Des Esseintes' eyes the concrete juice, the osmazone of literature, the essential oil of art.[22]

"Osmazone" is a word that Huysmans coined, akin to "umami," the fifth taste that is based in amino acids (mushrooms, meat, soy). The sense of concentrated meaning allies itself with poetry, of course, and the efficiency of figurative language.

## The Prose Poem and Dialogism

One of the features the prose poem shares with the novel is dialogism (also called heteroglossia), a term coined by Mikhail Bakhtin, a Russian structuralist at the beginning of the twentieth century. Bakhtin argues that, unlike the lyric poem, which foregrounds the unity of the speaking voice, the novel allows multiple language systems (sources of diction, dialects, tones, speech patterns) to clash against each other, producing a work that is unhegemonic and thus subversive. In other words, no one is "in charge" of the language, and pieces of language are "taken" (consciously or not) from all kinds of sources.[23] Jonathan Monroe, in *A Poverty of Objects: The Prose Poem and the Politics of Genre*, argues that the prose poem's simultaneous dialogism and displacement of the lyric subject result in a politically subversive form.[24] One of Baudelaire's prose poems, "Windows," shows dialogism at work, as well as its potential for political subversion. The poem can also be read as a critique of the realist novel.

*Windows*

When you look through an open window from the outside, you don't see as much as when you look at a closed window. Nothing is deeper, more mysterious, more fecund, more shadowy, more dazzling, than a window lit up by a candle. What you see in the sun is always less interesting than what happens behind a pane of glass. In that black and luminous hole, life lives, dreams, and suffers.

Over the waving rooftops, I see an old woman, wrinkled,
  poor, bent over something, a woman who never goes out.
  Using her face, using her clothing, using almost nothing,
  I rewrote the story of her life, or rather her legend, and
  sometimes I tell it to myself and cry.

If it had been a poor old man, I would have rewritten his just
  as easily.
And I go to bed, proud of having lived and suffered in
  others.
Perhaps you will say to me: "Are you sure that that legend is
  true?" What does it matter what reality might be outside
  of myself, if it helps me to live, to feel that I am and what
  I am?[25]

The speaker "rewrote the story of a poor, old woman's life," but
in a way that does not resemble novelistic narration. Neverthe-
less, as in the novels of Émile Zola or Honoré de Balzac, the
character in this imagined story is of a different class, gender,
and age than her creator. The speaker has made of her an "oth-
er," but uses empathy not only to convey the difficulties of her
life, but also "to feel that I am and what I am." In other words,
by writing about a person very different from himself in social
status, the storyteller distinguishes himself from those he writes
about. The complex tone is ironic, signaled by the speaker's
pride in "having lived and suffered in others."

The *open* window is a trope for the art of a novelist. In this
respect it is akin to the mirror. (In *The Red and the Black*, Stend-
hal defines the novel as a "mirror carried along a highway,"[26]
and George Eliot, in *Adam Bede*, calls her work "a faithful ac-
count of men and things as they have mirrored themselves in my
mind.")[27] By contrast, the *closed* window lit by a candle is a trope
for the art of the prose poet. There is no presumption of real-
ism, and the truth of the imagining is gauged by an emotional
response rather than mimesis. Moreover, the candlelight lends
an aura of mystery.

During the mid-nineteenth century, as the realist novel
gained hegemony, free verse and the prose poem were evolving
as new forms both in France and in England. In 1897, at the
same time that Arthur Rimbaud and Stéphane Mallarmé were

writing prose poems, http://www.piranesia.net/baudelaire/
spleen/34deja.htmlMallarmé was writing (very) free verse using
the page (right and left margins), typographical changes to im-
pact the reading process, and convoluted syntax. In his preface
to *A Throw of the Dice Will Never Eliminate Chance* (1897) Mallarmé
writes:

> The ensuing words, laid out as they are, lead on to the last,
> with no novelty except the spacing of the text. The "blanks"
> indeed take on importance, at first glance; the versification
> demands them, as a surrounding silence, to the extent that
> a fragment, lyrical or of a few beats, occupies, in its midst, a
> third of the space of paper: I do not transgress the measure,
> only disperse it. . . . The literary value, if I am allowed to say
> so, of this print-less distance which mentally separates groups
> of words or words themselves, is to periodically accelerate or
> slow the movement, the scansion, the sequence even, given
> one's simultaneous sight of the page: the latter taken as unity,
> as elsewhere the Verse is or perfect line.[28]

Both the novel and the prose poem depend on the *printed page*
and are forms for (mostly) solitary enjoyment. Robert Bly notes
about this intimacy, "We often feel in a prose poem a man or a
woman talking not before a crowd, but in a low voice to some-
one he is sure is listening."[29]

One might see free verse as an intermediary form between
prose and verse. It became popular around the same time as
the prose poem, although Blake, Shelley, Matthew Arnold, and
many other poets used free verse before its dominant period in
the twentieth century. H. T. Kirby Smith offers examples of free
verse in the oeuvre of poets both known and unknown (as early
as Barnabe Barnes in 1593) and argues that metrical variations
were often, as in the case of John Milton in *Samson Agonistes*,
more dominant than metrical adherence.[30] The biblical or bard-
ic form of free verse has had many practitioners: before Walt
Whitman, there was Martin Farquhar Tupper, whose very popu-
lar (especially in England) 1837 *Proverbial Philosophy* was written
in free verse. Interestingly, today Tupper's work is usually consid-
ered "bad" because it is seen as didactic and because the lines,
despite being cut up, read like prose.[31] In short, at the same time

143

that the prose poem is flourishing, so is free verse. They might be said to come from the same impulses; they both challenge form and genre and permit the creation of more hybrids.

## Translation

In addition to links to the realist novel and to free verse, the prose poem's genome can also be traced from issues of translation. Sometimes translators can convey both content and form of poems, but often content is more important, as in, for example, Charles Singleton's prose translations of Dante's *Divine Comedy*. Vista Clayton points out that famous French translations of Latin, Greek, English, and Italian verse (i.e., Bonaventure des Periers' 1543 translation of Horace; Madame Dacier's translation of Anacreon and Sappho in 1681, and the *Iliad* in 1711) were prose, and that this movement introduced the reading public to literature that gained its texture from the sentence as opposed to the line.[32] Subsequent prose translations of the Hebrew Bible (much of which is originally in verse) have been termed "poetry." For example, here's Fénelon on the Bible: "Nothing else equals the magnificence and the sweep of the Songs of Moses. The Book of Job is a poem full of tropes, bold and majestic. . . . The writing is full of poetry at the same time that it is devoid of versification."[33]

## The French Prose Poem

France is regarded as the home of the prose poem, partly because of the fame of Baudelaire, and also because the hybrid form achieved legitimacy there sooner than in England, the United States, or Germany. Michael Delville notes that the rigidity of French rhyme and verse made France a likely home for a revolt.[34] The surreal content of nineteenth- and twentieth-century prose poems has a precursor in Charles Nodier's 1821 *Smarra*, a work described by Vista Clayton as "fantastic creations of the imagination when it is freed by sleep"—in other words, nightmares.[35] Nodier is a less-known precursor to Aloysius Bertrand, and Bertrand is a less-known precursor to Baudelaire.

The prose poems in Bertrand's 1842 *Gaspard de la Nuit* feature a rich lexicon. The pieces are hard to place, historically: some seem medieval, some Renaissance, some impossible to place in any particular time. If the realist novel is anchored in history, it seems the prose poem plays with history, or ignores it. "What is art?" asks Bertrand, and then answers, "Art is the science of the poet."[36] The melding of art and science is reflected in the subtitle of the collection, *Fantasies in the Manner of Rembrandt and Callot*. Although *Gaspard de la Nuit* is broken into sections, it really works only as a whole—not a novel, but a whole *something*. It can't be excerpted. Some titles suggest the descriptive focus of the poems: "The Night Beggar," "The Tulip Merchant," "The Sabbath Hour," "The Five Fingers of the Hand." Bertrand's poems, written when he was twenty-two, are more hermetic than those of Baudelaire. They're also hard to translate, probably another reason the book isn't well known.

Charles Baudelaire not only read Bertrand but acknowledged his work in the introduction to his posthumously published 1869 *Le Spleen de Paris* (subtitle: *Petit Poèmes en Prose*). Baudelaire's poems are set in his contemporary Paris and share some of the same themes as his infamous book of lineated poems, *Les Fleurs du Mal*. Baudelaire often critiques class hierarchies, as replicated in the modern city (hence, the title). The introduction to the prose poems, addressed to Arsène Houssaye, contains a passage oft-cited as a battle cry for the prose poem: "Which one of us, in his moments of ambition, has not dreamed of the miracle of a poetic prose, musical, without rhythm and without rhyme, supple enough and rugged enough to adapt itself to the lyrical impulses of the soul, the undulations of reverie, the jibes of conscience?"[37]

The yearning for "supple" and "rugged" suggests the difficulties poets faced when trying to fit new ideas into the rigid nineteenth-century forms. The freedom to think outside convention is of course an aspect of all art and every kind of poem, but Baudelaire has a special anarchy of the spirit, considering the conventions of his era. To love clouds more than anything or anyone else is freedom from social bonds, but Baudelaire also gave writers the license to surrealism and to Dada. Some poems in the collection are fables ("The Dog and the Perfume Bottle"), others are stories with a strange and cruel reversal, still others offer advice like "Get Drunk." Baudelaire's prose poems are structured variously; most are narrative, some are arguments, others are descriptions. Their sentiments may be revolutionary, but each of them is structured tightly and clearly: there is no doubt how they work. And interestingly, none of them contain particularly dense or complicated language or surreal imagery.

We can see the anarchy of spirit in the first of Baudelaire's poems in *Le Spleen de Paris*, "The Stranger," a dialogue:

> Tell me, enigmatic man, whom do you love the best? Your
>     father, your mother, your sister, or your brother?
> —I have neither father, nor mother, nor sister, nor brother.
> —Your friends?
> —I don't know what "friends" are.
> —Your country?
> —I don't know where to find it.
> —Beauty?
> —I would love to love her, that immortal goddess.
> —Gold?
> —I hate it as much as you hate God.
> —Well then! What do you love, extraordinary stranger?
> —I love the clouds . . . the passing clouds . . . over there . . .
>     over there . . . the marvelous clouds![38]

The diction and syntax in the representative poems "Windows" and "The Stranger" are simple and lend an informal tone. Even at the age of twenty, I could translate the French. So it seems that while "richness" of language is often cited as a characteristic of the prose poem, Baudelaire's poems don't have it. Perhaps the simplicity—shall we call it "elegance"?—of these prose poems has contributed to their dissemination and translatability.

# Tone in the Prose Poem

Because of the formal restrictions of verse, by comparison prose tends to seem more informal and closer to conversation. We have also seen that prose is "faster." If tone is the speaker's attitude toward the subject, how then do informality and speed affect the tone of a prose poem? To explore the differences between lineated and unlineated verse, let us examine a prose poem by Anne Carson from her first book, *Short Talks*, the publisher's blurb of which reads as follows:

> Lyric sermons: Riddle-poems that consist only of answers: Lou Reed meets Claude Monet and converts to Zen: The pure hilarious ache of ontology: *Short Talks* is elegiac, perceptive, droll. It is the first book-length collection by an accomplished, original voice. Sunday mornings are never going to be the same again.

The parataxis of this blurb echoes the parataxis of the poems, but note that the blurb doesn't mention the *prose form* of the poems; rather, it takes it for granted. First, the poem in prose:

*Short Talk on Reading*

Some fathers hate to read but love to take the family on
    trips. Some children hate trips but love to read. Funny
    how often these find themselves passengers in the same
    automobile. I glimpsed the stupendous clear cut shoul-
    ders of the Rockies from between paragraphs of *Madame
    Bovary*. Cloud shadows roved languidly across her huge
    rock throat, traced her fir flanks. Since those days I do
    not look at hair on female flesh without thinking, Decidu-
    ous?[39]

Now, the poem lineated (by me):

Some fathers hate to read
but love to take the family on trips. Some children
hate trips but love to read. Funny how often
these find themselves passengers in the same
automobile. I glimpsed the stupendous clear

cut shoulders of the Rockies from between
paragraphs of *Madame Bovary*. Cloud shadows roved
languidly across her huge rock throat, traced her fir
flanks. Since those days I do not look at hair
on female flesh without thinking,
Deciduous?

When lineated, it seems the poem takes itself too seriously. It is, after all, a "short talk" that melds reading and car trips through the humorous image of mountains as a female body, the trees being the hair. Most of the poems in Carson's collection are humorous, whether tonally dark or light. Speed contributes to the humor.

We see that prose is read more rapidly than lines of verse, with the result that prose *seems* more modest. As Mallarmé theorized about the expansion of white space, the contraction of white space has the opposite effect. The poet is using the form of "plain folks." The apparent implication is that anyone can write prose, although (of course) not everyone can write a good prose poem. Robert Bly notes that "the prose poem is the final stage of the unpretentious style . . . useful for renewing the narrative, and for expressing complicated human perceptions."[40] Similarly, the poems of Francis Ponge, *Proêmes* (1948) and *The Voice of Things* (*Le parti pris des Choses*) (1942), seem unpretentious because they are grounded in ordinary things. In a sense, Ponge's prose poems, along with those of Max Jacob, have become templates for U.S. practitioners of the prose poem. Below is my translation of Ponge's "The Pleasures of the Door":

*The Pleasures of the Door*

Kings do not touch doors.
They don't know that pleasure: to push gently or brusquely a
 large familiar panel, then turn around to put it back—to
 hold it in one's arms.

The pleasure of grabbing the porcelain knot of its belly,
 of turning an obstacle into an entry. A quick grappling
 during which you stop for a second, open your eyes, and
 your whole body fits into a new place.

With a friendly hand you hold it a second longer before
   pushing it back and shutting yourself in—confirmed by
   the click of the powerful and well-oiled spring.[41]

The most radical incarnation of the prose poem in any
language is probably Gertrude Stein's *Tender Buttons* (1914).
Her domestic subjects are divided into "Objects," "Food," and
"Rooms." Some are a few sentences long, some are three or four
pages long. Here's an example:

*MILK.*

A white egg and a colored pan and a cabbage showing
   settlement, a constant increase.

A cold in a nose, a single cold nose makes an excuse. Two
   are more necessary.

All the goods are stolen, all the blisters are in the cup.

Cooking, cooking is the recognition between sudden and
   nearly sudden very little and all large holes.

A real pint, one that is open and closed and in the middle is
   so bad.

Tender colds, seen eye holders, all work, the best of change,
   the meaning, the dark red, all this and bitten, really
   bitten.

Guessing again and golfing again and the best men, the very
   best men.

MILK.

Climb up in sight climb in the whole utter needles and a
   guess a whole guess is hanging. Hanging hanging.[42]

Stein torques syntax at the same time that she removes words
from their usual contexts. As far as mode, the poems might best
be termed arguments (against patriarchy). Stein's focus on ob-

jects is subversive because it makes us question our relation to the nouns that represent them.

Michael Delville examines other U.S. writers of the prose poem, among them Arturo Giovannitti, Carl Sandburg, Sherwood Anderson, and Kenneth Patchen.[43] Many contemporary poets have also tried their hand at the prose poem, most famously Russell Edson, Charles Simic, Mark Strand, and James Tate, but also Anne Waldman, Rosmarie Waldrop, and Karen Volkman.

Finally, here is a poem that has me questioning the form of the prose poem yet again, Ann Killough's "Statue of Liberty"

> And yet we suspect that our relationship to the Statue of
>     Liberty is
> not simple.
>
> That we are expecting something from her which she is
>     secretly no
> longer providing.
>
> That she is actually undermining our entire sense of
>     ourselves, not
> only collectively but individually.
>
> What do you think?
>
> I mean really.
>
> No fair coming up with that stuff about the symbol of our
>     nation or
> our nation's delusions about its own saintly welcoming
>     qualities or
> anything to do with France.
>
> Think in terms of if aliens had already contacted the Statue
>     of Liberty and
> she were receiving transmissions across the whole surface of
>     her copper
> body which she were greatly enjoying after all those years of
>     nothing but

runny condensations.

Think in terms of what the aliens might have in mind.

Would they care that she was hollow and full of stairs?

Would they care that she was too big to be happy?

\*

So now what if the Statue of Liberty has found out that she
    can move
and is only waiting for the right moment?

What if there are beginning to be words in her book, more
    and
more words on the coppery pages, the ones that do not turn,
    or not
yet?

What if she is beginning to feel the horror of her position,
    the way
she has no peers or anyone who understands that she is in
    the
tradition of the enormous destroyer?

What is it she is coming convinced she must destroy?

\*

So now picture what you think the Statue of Liberty might
    destroy
and realize that you are not right.

That whatever you thought of is not it, or at least not quite it
    and
certainly not all of it.

That you have no idea what she is thinking, or at least not a
    complete
idea.

That the very nature of her body renders her susceptible not
    only to
alien transmissions but to all the transmissions of the earth.

That she is a kind of Pole along with the North and South
    ones and
draws the magnetic fields of the earth toward herself like
    shiploads
of huddled immigrants and reads them like ticker tape
    inside her
spiky head.

That she feels what you feel but much more of it.

That she sees what you see but the backside of it as well, the
    side
you will never see.

That she has already begun to change something even in
    you, even
in me.

That we already know what it is.[44]

Note that the above passage features extremely long lines that
are deliberately broken, rather than determined by the end of
the page. Like St.-John Perse's *Anabasis*, Killough mixes long
lines and stanzas broken for pauses. The poem is difficult to
excerpt because it works by accretion. Its conversational, con-
templative tone is not at all like Jacob's or Ponge's compressed
attention to the physical world. Nor is it like Baudelaire's narra-
tives. Still, like many prose poems, Killough's "Statue of Liberty"
features a dissatisfaction with the status quo.

The poem begins in the middle, with the phrase "and yet,"
suggesting that a whole chapter (indeed a whole book) has pre-
ceded the moment of the poem. It then slides into its various
rhetorical strategies. For instance, the repeated openings of the
sentences, "what if" in the second section and "that" in the last
section, recall a manifesto. In 2007 I asked Ann Killough about
this form in an e-mail. She replied:

I think the form mostly came out of a kind of obsession, a determination to pick up a thread of the terrible tangle that is our national discourse and pull and pull and not stop until I got somewhere or got hopelessly lost, which was more like it. I think there was often a determination to get lost. As if I wouldn't find anything real unless or until I got lost. I didn't think so much in terms of lines as of paragraphs, with the rhythm of those, the places you choose to end each one, the kinds of spaces between them. Maybe that's the difference between prose poetry and poems with really long lines? I think of regular poetry as suspended from its lines and line breaks, swinging gracefully or not down the page as if on vertical monkey bars. Whereas the paragraphs in *Beloved Idea* are just going and going until they aren't. Like one of those old-timey hardcore punk bands (I'm thinking of Minor Threat or Fugazi) who play like a bat out of hell and then stop BAM! and then start again and then stop BAM again. There's Faulkner, too, of course, always, with that sense that the interminable sentence, or series of sentences, is the unit of exploration into the heart of our national grief and darkness.[45]

The prose poem allows the writer to "get lost," while a poem in verse requires a certain degree of retrieval. The moment of finding or retrieval suggests stasis and certainty, notions antithetical to art as process. I think Killough's mentioning punk bands from the 1980s is significant: It marks the prose poem's ability to absorb influences and to hybridize. Killough gets to have it both ways in *Beloved Idea*: her poems have the "just folks" attitude of prose—an attitude suitable to a citizen interrogating the politics of her country. But they are also artful, in that the lines are broken, not by the end of the page, but by the poet. The frequent pauses between paragraphs give the reader the time and space to absorb and consider what has been said, but they also suggest the difficulty of saying anything at all.

The hegemony of the realist novel and its faithful mirror continues—reincarnated perhaps in the form of first-person memoir. At the same time it has abundantly produced its "counterform," the prose poem. As Russell Edson understood, the prose poem is a hybrid animal that in turn makes us consider the living, animal nature of literary genres. The prose poem shows us that art is both plastic and inbred—relying on what has gone before, but enervating itself in the new.

*Notes*

1. Russell Edson, "The Prose Poem as a Beautiful Animal," in *Best of the Prose Poem: An International Journal* (Buffalo, NY: White Pine Press, 2000). Reprinted with permission by the author.

2. Michael Riffaterre, "On the Prose Poem's Formal Features," in *The Prose Poem in France: Theory and Practice* (New York: Colombia University Press, 1983), 117–132.

3. David Lehman, "The Prose Poem: An Alternative to Verse," *American Poetry Review* 32, no. 2 (March–April 2003), 45.

4. Suzanne Bernard, *Le poem en prose de Baudelaire a nos jours* (Paris: Nizet, 1959).

5. Novalis, "Hymns to the Night," in *Rampolli: Growths from a Long-Planted Root*, trans. George McDonald (London: Longmans, Green, 1897), Project Gutenberg Ebook.

6. Gustave Flaubert, "Letter to Louise Colet," in *The Letters of Gustave Flaubert*, vols. 1 and 2, *1830–1880*, ed. and trans. Francis Steegmuller (London: Picador/Macmillan, 2001), 288.

7. Stéphane Mallarmé, interview from *Enquête sur l'évolution littéraire*, ed. Jules Huret (Charleston, SC: BiblioBazaar, 1891), University of Duisburg-Esse Online texts.

8. Ron Silliman, *The New Sentence* (New York: Roof Books, 1977), 91.

9. Stephen Fredman, *Poet's Prose: The Crisis in American Verse*, 2nd ed. (Cambridge: Cambridge University Press, 1990), 80.

10. Max Jacob, *The Dice Cup* (New York: Sun, 1979), 7.

11. Saint-John Perse, *Anabasis*, trans. T. S. Eliot (New York: Harcourt, Brace, 1949), 11.

12. Perse, *Anabasis*.

13. Paul Valéry, *The Art of Poetry*, trans. Denise Folliot (Princeton: Princeton University Press, 1985), 207.

14. Gertrude Stein, "Poetry and Grammar," in *Writings, 1932–1946* (New York: Library of America, 1998), 327.

15. Peter Johnson, "An Interview with Russell Edson," *Writer's Chronicle* 31, no 6 (1999), 30–36.

16. Charles Simic, *Unemployed Fortune-Teller* (Ann Arbor: University of Michigan Press, 1995), 118.

17. Ian Watt, *The Rise of the Novel: Studies in Defoe, Richardson, and Fielding*, 2nd ed. (Berkeley: University of California Press, 2001).

18. Margueritte Murphy, *A Tradition of Subversion: The Prose Poem in English from Wilde to Ashbery* (Amherst: University of Massachusetts Press, 1992).

19. Saint-John Perse, *Letters*, trans. Arthur J. Knodel (Princeton: Princeton University Press, 1978), 492.

20. Catherine Belsey, *Critical Practice* (London: Routledge, 1990).

21. Calvin Bedient, "The Predicament of Modern Poetry (The Lyric at the Pinch-Gate)," *Chicago Review* 51–52, no. 4/1 (Spring 2006), 135–54.

22. Joris Karl Huysmans, *Against the Grain (A rebours)*, trans. S. Mac-Gregor Mathers (New York: Dover, 1969), 186.

23. Mikhail Bakhtin, *The Dialogic Imagination*, ed. Michael Holquist, trans. Caryl Emerson and Michael Holquist (Austin: University of Texas Press, 1981).

24. Jonathan Monroe, *A Poverty of Objects: The Prose Poem and the Politics of Genre* (Ithaca: Cornell University Press, 1987).

25. Charles Baudelaire, "Les Fenêtres," in *Le Spleen de Paris: Petits Poèmes en Prose* (Paris: Livre de Poche, 1972), 139; my translation.

26. Stendhal, *The Red and the Black*, trans. Stirling Haig (Cambridge: Cambridge University Press, 1989), 43.

27. George Eliot, *Adam Bede* (New York: Signet Classics, 2004), Read Print Edition, chap. 17.

28. Stéphane Mallarmé, "Mallarmé: Un coup de dés jamais n'abolira le hasard: A throw of the dice will never abolish chance," *Wiki-Source*, August 31, 2012, http://fr.wikisource.org/wiki/Un_coup_de_d%C3%A9s_jamais_n%E2%80%99abolira_le_hasard.

29. Robert Bly, "What the Prose Poem Carries with It," *American Poetry Review* 6, no. 3 (1977), 45.

30. H. T. Kirby-Smith, *The Origins of Free Verse* (Ann Arbor: University of Michigan Press, 1996).

31. Martin Farquhar Tupper, *Proverbial Philosophy* (Philadelphia: Herman Hooker, 1845).

32. Vista Clayton, *The Prose Poem in French Literature of the Eighteenth Century* (New York: Columbia University Press, 1936),7,27.

33. Clayton, *Prose Poem*, 7.

34. Michel Delville, *The American Prose Poem: Poetic Form and the Boundaries of Genre* (Gainesville: University Press of Florida), 1998.

35. Clayton, *Prose Poem*, 117.

36. Aloysius Bertrand, *Gaspard de la Nuit: Fantaisies à la Manière de Rembrandt et de Calot* (Paris: Flammarion, 1972), 37.

37. Charles Baudelaire, *Paris Spleen*, trans. Louise Varèse (New York: New Directions, 1970), ix–x.

38. Charles Baudelaire, "The Stranger" in *Le Spleen de Paris: Petits Poèmes en Prose* (Paris: Livre de Poche, 1972), 29; my translation.

39. Anne Carson, "Short Talk on Reading," in *Short Talks* (London, Ontario: Brick Books, 1992), 41. Reprinted with permission by the author.

40. Robert Bly, *News of the Universe: Poems of Twofold Consciousness* (Berkeley: University of California Press, 1995), 131.

41. Francis Ponge, "Les plaisirs de la porte," *Paire D'as*, August 31, 2012, http://www.pairedas.net/joomla/content-all-comcontent-views/category-list/77-les-plaisirs-de-la-porte.html.

42. Gertrude Stein, "Food. Stein, Gertrude. 1914. Tender Buttons," *Bartleby: Great Books Online*, August 2010, http://www.bartleby.com/140/2.html.

43. Delville, *American Prose Poem*.

44. Ann Killough, "Statue of Liberty," in *Beloved Idea* (Farmington, ME: Alice James Books, 2007), 27–29. Reprinted with the permission of The Permissions Company, Inc., on behalf of Alice James Books, www.alicejamesbooks.org.

45. Ann Killough, e-mail correspondence to Natasha Sajé.

# Dynamic Design

### *The Structure of Books of Poems*

A collection of poems is sequential, not simultaneous like visual art, but many times when readers open a book, they don't read the poems in the order they have been arranged. Does it matter, then, how a book of poems is organized? What goes into the shaping of a book, and what is the effect of that shaping on the reader?

Even though many poets organize their poems into books intuitively, and even though readers may be highly disparate in their practices, I think it does matter how a book of poems is organized. In fact, I like to think of a book's organization as its "gesture" (from Latin, "to carry")—how the book *carries* itself to a reader, and how the reader responds to that gesture.

Poets have long had a hand in structuring their books of poems. In *Poems in Their Place*, Neil Fraistat lists Ovid, Horace, Petrarch, Virgil, Milton, Pope, Dickinson, Whitman, and Yeats as poets known to have paid attention to what Fraistat terms "contexture," which he defines as "the contextuality provided for each poem by the larger frame within which it is placed, the intertextuality among poems so placed, and the resultant texture of resonance and meanings."[1] Robert Frost, C. P. Cavafy, Adelaide Crapsey, and Wallace Stevens are modern poets whose contextuality within the collection revealed new insights about their work. In the case of Sylvia Plath's *Ariel*, Marjorie Perloff shows that the book organized by Ted Hughes emphasizes death and self-destruction, while the book as originally organized by Plath reveals her outrage at Hughes' adultery.[2] In their study of Edgar Lee Masters' *Spoon River Anthology*, John Berryman's *Dream Songs*, and Robert Lowell's *Life Studies*, among others, M.

L. Rosenthal and Sally Gall argue that the modern poetic sequence "fulfills the need for encompassment of disparate and often powerfully opposed tonalities and energies"[3] through a "liberated lyrical structure."[4] We know that structure does indeed complicate meaning, and in questioning *how* it does, we might draw upon Roland Barthes' notions of *writerly* and *readerly* texts. Has the poet created a text that allows the reader maximum possibility? Barthes insists that "the goal of literary work (of literature as work) is to make the reader no longer a consumer, but a producer of the text."[5] Writerly texts allow "entrances, the opening of networks, the infinity of languages."[6] For his purposes in *The Pleasure of the Text,* he uses analogous terms: the text of *pleasure* and the text of *bliss.* For Barthes, the text of pleasure "contents, fills, grants euphoria; comes from culture and does not break with it, is linked to a *comfortable* practice of reading." But the text of bliss is "the text that imposes a state of loss, the text that discomforts," that "unsettles the reader's historical, cultural, psychological assumptions, . . . [and] brings to a crisis his relation with language."[7] If the text of pleasure is a marriage, then the text of bliss gestures like lover.

But the terms readerly/pleasure and writerly/bliss ought not be taken as synonyms for oppositional terms of "conventional/classical" versus "experimental/avant-garde." It is especially important to note that the latter category *is created by the reader.* "The writerly text is not a thing," Barthes points out,[8] but a "perpetual present." Criticism treats texts of pleasure, while bliss is beyond words. Thus Barthes' terms do not signify binary oppositions between easy and difficult or between mainstream and avant-garde. In fact, the writerly text cannot be found in the bookstore,[9] but is rather a process of reading, a questioning of convention. Barthes' provocative ideas emphasize the ineffability of the *reader's* production of the text, and its personal, even onanistic nature.

We can examine the conventions that apply to the structure of books of poetry, and in so doing discover how they carry one over the threshold (or not) into bliss. An outline of these conventions—writerly gestures, if you will, contained in readerly texts—will be useful to both reader and poet. Readers more alert to these conventions will be better able to construct their own bliss in the books of poems on their shelves. Poets will be better prepared to consider these gestures when putting together their next books. Since my aim is to convey the range of principles of organization, my treatment of them is necessarily glancing.

The beginning of a book tells the reader a great deal about what will follow. With what gestures do poets welcome readers into their worlds? Opening strategies can seize the reader's attention, enacting a sense of mystery or anticipation, beginning, dawn, birth, or creation, signaling the book as the new thing that it is. For example, Veronica Patterson begins her book *Swan, What Shores?* with a poem ending on "Sometimes, unguarded, you fall asleep"—a suggestion that what follows is the unguarded product of a dream world. Carl Phillips begins *Cortège* with "The Compass," a poem that ends on "what is lovely an arrow"— an arrow itself, pointing to the following poems.

Generally speaking, poets seem to prefer opening their books with a shorter poem, as though they were presenting an appetizer. But there are plenty of exceptions to that convention. See for example, books by Campbell McGrath, Carolyn Forché, and Heather McHugh, among others, books that open with longer poems, perhaps signaling the poet's seriousness and ambition, and implying that the reader is hungry enough to start right in on the main course.

The autobiographical strategy—or perhaps we should remain with the term "gesture"—introduces the reader to the speaker of the poems, often opening the book as a narrative of the speaker's life. For example, Sharon Olds opens *The Gold Cell* with "I Go Back to 1937," a poem that is a flashback in time to the speaker's parents, thereby signaling her psychoanalytic interest in herself as a product of her parents. Martìn Espada opens *A Mayan Astronomer in Hell's Kitchen* with "My Name is Espada," taking a different spin on the autobiographical by invoking the historical, etymological wordplay of his name, and by embracing an ethnic family larger than his two parents. The autobiographical gesture negotiates between self and subject; that is, the poet is never just a unique person speaking honestly about her individual life, but is rather someone subject to social codes that include class, race, nationality, and gender. Moreover, because the poet uses language, which is also subject to these

159

codes, saying "I" is doubly vexed. No self is primary, untouched by culture—and poets acknowledge this to varying degrees.

Some autobiographical gestures remain deliberately oblique—in effect the poet is saying, "Don't expect this to be a memoir, because 'I' can't be contained in a poem." Sandra Alcosser begins *Except by Nature* with "My Number," a poem of twelve couplets functioning as a biography of an alter ego. The poet's number is "small. A hundred pounds of water." The speaker "wears her like a shadow" and they "judge each other." The poem ends with "Together we dance—my number and her best dresses." Using the term "number" to signify an alter ego plays against the infinite nature of personality, which of course can't be summed up with mere numbers. Yet the poet's number—which *can* be made concrete in language—is also the book that follows, in a dance with the reader.

Lucie Brock-Broido begins *The Master Letters* with "Carrowmore," an oblique autobiographical gesture: "Wherever I went I came with me . . . My thick braid, my ornament— // My belonging I / Remember how cold I will be." She seems to speak for poets who question the easy correlation of identity and biography, who create poetry as alternative autobiography, using convention but giving it a writerly turn. In other words, the "facts" may not be there, but poems, like fingerprints, still provide a sense of the poet's identity.

Another version of the autobiographical gesture is a poem "about" seeing. In a sense, a book takes the reader on a tour of what the poet sees—or doesn't see. Thus, poems about seeing often include disclaimers, presenting the problems of subjectivity, light, and point of view. Heather McHugh begins her first book, *Dangers*, with "Spectacles," a poem that notes how subjective seeing is, that each of us sees what she wants to see. A pair of spectacles can be a "bright suggestion to the uncorrected / eye, or a small / wrecked bicycle." Likewise, the first poem in Robert Hass' *Praise* is "Heroic Smile," a poem that combines point of view with a disclaimer and begins with "A man and a woman walk from the movies / to the house in the silence of separate fidelities. / There are limits to imagination." And Charles Wright opens *Black Zodiac* with "Apologia Pro Vita Sua," a poem that ends with "more work to be done," a merging of the autobiographical with a disclaimer, a statement of the poet's insufficiency or inability. Harryette Mullen actually spoofs the convention of the disclaimer, opening *Sleeping with the Dictionary* with the prose poem "All She Wrote," which is a list of excuses for not writing: "Forgive me. I'm no good at this. I can't write back. I never read your letter. I can't say I got your note ... If I couldn't get back to writing, I thought I'd catch up on my reading. Then *Oprah* came on with a fabulous author plugging her best-selling book." Since Oprah doesn't read poetry, and books of poems don't become bestsellers, Mullen is claiming other territory for her poetry; in fact, the prose list functions like a photographic negative of a customary opening poem.

Poets sometimes begin their books with a prayer, a gesture that emphasizes the individual speaker as part of a larger community. Poets Agha Shahid Ali, Jorie Graham, Grace Schulman, Tom Sleigh, and Connie Voisine, among others, have opened their books with this gesture, suggesting that the book of poems is a religious experience, for the poet and hopefully for the reader. Recalling the Bible and other holy texts, the prayer places the poet in a tradition of the mystic or spiritual visionary or humble supplicant. Of course, what the poet *prays for* varies—independence for Kashmir in the case of Shahid Ali, for instance, or peace between Arabs and Jews in the case of Schulman. The reader is assumed to be part of a community that cares about the poet's plea. Conversely, Heather McHugh's seventeen-page deathbed vigil, "Not a Prayer," opens *The Father of the Predicaments* with a gesture of individual mourning.

Another conventional opening gesture is the *ars poetica*, a poem that calls attention to the genre of poetry itself by placing the poet among his (usually male) peers, and sometimes ironically. Mark Strand's list-poem, "The New Poetry Handbook," opens his book *Darker* ("If a man understands a poem, he shall have troubles"), creating a "club" for poets, making the male reader an honorary member. Gabriel Gudding's "A Defense of Poetry" opens his book of the same title with a nod to Philip Sidney's "Defence of Poesie" and Percy Shelley's "A Defence of Poetry." Gudding's poem takes the form of numbered prose statements, like Christopher Smart's "Jubilate Agno" about his cat Jeoffrey. Unlike Smart, who was actually confined to a madhouse, Gudding's speaker feigns madness, addressing a reader who has "the mental capacity of the Anchovy" and incorporating "discomfiting" references to bodily grossness. These gestures foreground the genre, perhaps compensating for the fact that poetry is not widely read, and that poets are not well known, something that would especially matter to male writers whose status in the culture can be diminished by writing poetry.

Yet another way to invite the reader is to begin with a poem about another art wherein the reader reads "poetry." Robert Hass opens *Human Wishes* with "Spring Drawing," and Seamus Heaney opens *The Spirit Level* with "The Rain Stick": "Who cares if all the music that transpires // Is the all of grit or dry seeds through a cactus? / You are a rich man entering heaven / Through the ear of a raindrop. Listen now again." And of course a broader—and much employed—version of the *ars poetica* is the poem about language itself.

Phillis Levin opens her book *Mercury* with "Part"—part personal poem of loss, part disclaimer, and part language poem— and in so doing combines several of these gestures. Levin's extended definition of the word "part" reminds the reader that both a poem and a book of poems are only pieces of a poet's work and self: "Of something, separate, not / Whole; a role, something to play / While one is separate or parting." The use of fragments and enjambed lines underscores the reader's partial story, and the last line's inversion—which leaves it without a period—asks the reader to supply the missing last word, "part":

Take from, sever, as in
Lord, part me from him,
I cannot bear to ever

Ancillary to a discussion of openings is a discussion of endings. What is the book's trajectory? How does the ending connect to the beginning? In the same way that a poem's ending holds the key to its interpretation, the last poem in a book underscores its meaning emphatically. Ideally, teleology (the study of endings) should seem inevitable from the beginning. Does the book click shut or hang in the air, dissolve or fly away? In the end (pun intended), no matter what tone it adopts, the last poem must *conclude*.

The same gestures that apply to beginnings apply to endings as well. For instance, Mark Doty begins *and* ends *Source* with an *ars poetica*. Some endings are self-conscious, for instance "Some Final Words" in Billy Collins' *The Art of Drowning* (an analogue to his opening poem, "Dear Reader"). Some books use a period of time as container and close with a poem about night; others return to some aspect of the opening gesture as a way of creating the book's wholeness. One of the most unusual instances of this is Linda McCarriston's *Eva Mary*, which begins and ends with the same poem, "The Apple Tree." Of course, after the intervening poems about domestic abuse and violence, the apple tree becomes a symbol of the fallen world. In David Baker's *Changeable Thunder*, clouds are the subject of the first and last poems, but the first poem is historical while the last poem personalizes clouds, almost as if the reader has earned this intimacy.

As we have seen, the idea of closure meets with some resistance in postmodern poetry, which has its antipathies to fixed meaning. Barbara Herrnstein Smith points out that "anti-closure is a recognizable impulse in all contemporary art, and at its furthest reaches it reflects changing presumptions concerning the nature of art itself."[10] Antiteleological art correlates with modern philosophy via an unfinished quality that suggests possibility, openness, continuation, an inability to determine endings, and skepticism. In the postmodern world where "conviction is seen as self-delusion and all last words are lies, the only resolution may be in the affirmation of irresolution, and conclusiveness may be seen as not only less honest but less stable than inconclusiveness."[11] Lyn Hejinian explains her resistance to closure another way:

> I perceive the world as vast and overwhelming; each moment stands under an enormous vertical and horizontal pressure of information, potent with ambiguity, meaning-full, unfixed, and certainly incomplete. What saves this from becoming a vast undifferentiated mass of date and situation is one's ability to make distinctions. Each written text may act as a distinction, may be a distinction. The experience of feeling over-

whelmed by undifferentiated material is like claustrophobia. One feels panicky, closed in. The open text is one which both acknowledges the vastness of the world and is formally differentiating. It is the form that opens it, in that case.[12]

Yet because poetry uses language—and language is structural—poets cannot *not* end their poems, or their books. Thus, the effect of anticlosure is bound to be subtle. Online poetry is an exception, because it is able to create an endless loop that doesn't permit the reader to get out, or to provide alternative endings. For instance, Stephanie Strickland's online poem *http://vniverse. com* demands more flexible reading than a traditional text. Some readers, unused to having their choices made so explicit, may find the poem more difficult or time consuming than a page-bound series of poems, yet this may well be the future of reading, and it certainly fulfills Roland Barthes' wish for a writerly text, one that the reader produces.

Asking contemporary poets how they begin the process of ordering the poems in their books produces a surprisingly uniform group of answers. The principles of structure that are generally mentioned include balance and contrast; dynamic energy; surprise; breathing space / white space; a dialogue between intent and serendipity, or in Annie Finch's words, between "tension and inevitability."[13] Here is the poet Elaine Terranova on the topic:

> For me putting a manuscript together is a reductive process, somewhat the way I write a poem. I'm always flinging poems aside, once I'm convinced that they "do not get along well with the others." The chosen poems form some sort of association. I'm looking for something that fits together organically, like a poem, just as in a poem I search for the lines that adhere. I feel a book should have distinct openings and closings. I'd begin with a poem about fresh starts, beginnings, mornings. Something that heralds the theme of the collection, something I'm setting out to prove. I remember how we'd pick a photo for a front page of the little newspaper I once worked for, that faced right, looking in to the rest of the paper.[14]

Alicia Ostriker says she puts a book together when she has more poems than necessary for a book-length collection: "The floor gets covered with poems grouped into various categories, regrouped, sequenced, exchanged with each other; the order shifts and reshifts, the sections of the book form and change places."[15] As Terranova points out, heuristics for organizing a manuscript can come from other genres. Poets can use film conventions to talk about movement. They can make jump cuts, and employ flashbacks, and develop a character, as Mary Jo Bang does in *Louise in Love*.

Another strategy is to move from the specific to general or the general to the specific—Does the book turn from a microscope to a telescope or vice versa? Susan Stewart's *The Forest* is divided into two parts, the first using personal and family material, and the second broadening or globalizing these concerns. As for the principle of structure in my own first book, *Red Under the Skin*, perhaps because I was teaching so much composition at the time, my method was rhetorical. I grouped the poems around three questions probably not apparent to a reader: how are we written upon? what can we do about it? how do we write back?

Just as we question beginnings and endings, and the movement between them, we can ask how poems are grouped within the book to create gestures. The way the end of one poem slides into or contrasts with the beginning of the next creates an associational order. These transitions can be thought of in terms of sequence, time, comparison, contrast, example, cause and effect, place, concession, summary, and repetition. For example, in Molly McQuade's *Barbarism*, the poem "Furtive and Fiery" ends with the line "in deciduous caves," while the next poem begins, "When a bear comes out at last into the woods." The transition is created by *place*: although the first poem mentions caves, it is not about bears, and the second poem elides the word "cave"; thus the space between the two poems creates the reader's momentary "cave."

One of the most amusing ways of ordering the poems in a book is an abecedary, where the poems are arranged alphabetically by title, as in Sharon Bryan's *Flying Blind*; Edward Kleinschmidt Mayes' *Works and Days*; Barbara Greenberg's *The Spoils of August*; Susan Stewart's *Columbarium*; and Harryette Mullen's *Sleeping with the Dictionary*. Other poets use an abecedary as an organizing principle for a section of their books, for instance

Barbara Hamby's *The Alphabet of Desire.* Although arrangement by alphabet is as old as the Psalms, its incarnation in contemporary poetry is postmodern, emphasizing randomness by allowing language rather than theme to dominate. In other words, if the poet arranges the poems alphabetically after they have all been titled, then the order is not dictated by content (although of course one could cheat and change titles to make the poems fit a secondary scheme).

Another way of ordering "randomly" is to use the *I Ching* (or to throw the poems down a flight of stairs?) to find mysterious and previously hidden resonances. I have yet to find someone who admits to doing this, but why not? As Stanley Fish notes in "Is There a Text in This Class?" the reader would still find order in such a random text, if only because it is our habit to assume some level of deliberation.[16] In other words, when one is primed to make meaning and see structure, one will. One might assume a flawed order, but never that there is no order whatsoever. When it comes to the element of chance, as Barbara Hernnstein Smith notes, we might consider the difference between playing a game and making art: "In games we 'play' with chance, in art we control chance."[17]

Yet another way of acknowledging chance is to order the poems in the book chronologically, by the date individual poems were written. Charles Wright admits to this method. "I know this is an odd process," he says, "but I have been doing it for years."[18] Although in most cases the reader has no way of knowing that the organizing principle is actually chronology, sometimes this method suggests an embedded narrative of self. In other words, as the poet grows and changes, so do the poems.

Sometimes it happens that a poet writes poems that adhere to particular groupings, thematic or formal, and then must decide whether to keep "groups" of like poems together or mix them up. The poet arranges the furniture of her house, deciding whether the experience needs *clarification* or *complication.* Recognizing poems grouped by theme and subject is easy because we are used to such groupings. We follow similar rules of organization every time we enter the grocery store. The danger is that the reader might become bored, expecting every poem in that group to be "about" family or jazz or food, and that the juxtapositions do not create energy. Readers expect to see a bed in the bedroom, while a bed in the kitchen can surprise. Poems grouped by theme should differ in other ways, in form or in tone, and serve the book as a whole.

In addition to the groupings themselves, sometimes marked by Roman numerals, the poet can offer another heuristic—that of section titles—which also must be held up to the same criterion as the rest of the book: does the section title highlight something that otherwise would be overlooked? The problem with such pointing is that titles can add to the wordage, insulting the reader's intelligence, akin to providing endnotes for already obvious information. Numbering the sections emphasizes sequence more than other kinds of markers, for instance asterisks. Dividing a book into sections is analogous to the division of an hour into quarters, a symphony into movements, a harmony into parts. But such divisions should make the experience more artful, not merely more clear.

A book that keeps groups of poems together is R. T. Smith's *Trespasser*, in which Ireland is the primary subject, but "Trespassing" with its etymology of "crossing" refers at once to the poet in a foreign land and the sins of humanity. Smith's book is divided into two sections: the first, "Uisce Beatha" (literally, "water of life" but colloquially, "whiskey"), is composed of twenty-six poems of daily life. The second, "Gristle," contains eleven poems of the miraculous, a series akin to Seamus Heaney's "Sweeney" poems. "Gristle" is cartilage, the substance that remains once the meat falls away. But Smith tells us that St. Gristle is a "shunned monk / shocked by Druid dolmens" whose church consists of "crickets, whin, and owl bones." The decision to group the "Gristle" poems together allows poems already so varied within themselves (in voice and subject) to be read together, thereby magnifying the pagan world they create. Had these poems been sprinkled throughout, the strong effect of ending the book with this group would have been lost. Coming as they do—together, at the end—the "Gristle" poems make the reader question the traditions and conventions detailed in the first section. The "Gristle" poems seem to say that there is a way out, a way through the imagination. Moreover, this smaller group suggests the lack of balance between the "real" and the "unreal," with the former being given considerably more space, but the latter being given the "last word."

A book that mixes groups is C. D. Wright's *Tremble*, constructed in a way that keeps the reader wondering what will come next. *Tremble* features thirty-six poems without subsections, appropriate for a short book of love poems. Wright sprinkles six "Girl Friend" poems—each dedicated to a different woman—throughout. The first is simply titled "Girl Friend," and it exemplifies Wright's gift for making her syntax surprising, and plumbing the possibilities of poetry by making the reader work in the white space. Following "Girl Friend" with a poem titled "And It Came to Pass" suggests that a community of voices and relationships provides the answer to the nature of "something else out there." The book closes with "Girl Friend Poem #6":

When I snap my fingers
You will wake in a dear yet unfamiliar place
You will scarcely remember your travail
You will be eating green caterpillars over a small fire
An awesome congeries of youthful men and women
Will be brushing these very tracks away.[19]

"Girl Friend Poem #6" exemplifies Wright's gift for inviting the reader into her life: the addressee is Debbie, but also the reader, whom the poet wakes out of the hypnotic state of reading and into the world. The poem ends the volume with a note of generosity and lightness, intimacy and otherworldliness, and Wright's attention to the nuance of sequence makes *Tremble* a construct of dynamic energy.

There is no appended list of explanatory or bibliographic notes in Wright's *Tremble*. But quite a few contemporary books of poems do contain appended material, in what I would argue is a "readerly" gesture. T. S. Eliot may have started the trend, appending notes to *The Waste Land* that Richard Badenhausen points out "seem to exclude the amateur unschooled in the proper use of such scholarly apparatuses."[20] Vladimir Nabokov's novel *Pale Fire* spoofed notes by giving them a life of their own, Paul Fournel wrote a novel composed entirely of footnotes. Now it seems some contemporary poets have also put pressure on the convention, for example Jenny Boully.

But the notes of most contemporary poets seem motivated by a desire to appear well read—or perhaps to save the reader trouble—and/or to dictate the reading of the particular poem. For instance, Adrienne Rich's "Six Narratives," in *Dark Fields of the Republic, Poems 1991–1995*, includes a note that says the narratives are spoken in different voices, information that could have been included in the title, signaled by the poems themselves, or simply left to the reader to decide. In the note to "Prayer" in *Never*, Jorie Graham writes, "I take my poem to be in conversation with such notion of the gods—and of how history transforms them—as is put forth in Herbert's poem. In attempting to enact a realistic description of metamorphosis, 'Prayer' wonders, among other things, what the 'suitable' distance between subject and object, gods and humans, humans and nature, might be."[21] That the poet gives the critics a head start suggests an uneasiness that they won't get there without her, either because the poem's text is obscure or because the critics are dense. One might recall again Barthes' quest for the writerly text, not as a license for obscurity, or justification of difficulty for its own sake, but for the reader's *bliss*. A book of poems is a space of play, and endnotes seem to close that space with a fence.

In a world where poems are more often than not read in anthologies, magazines, on the Web and out of their original context, it's important to be reminded of the ways context can enhance one's reading experience. While reading a poem in an anthology is like an air kiss, reading it within the structure the poet has provided for it can be a thoroughly sexual encounter. For me, Yusef Komunyakaa's *Talking Dirty to the Gods* epitomizes the writerly text. Indeed, its very project argues that language is a kind of sexual pleasure. The book contains 132 (the large number creates an orgy!) poems consisting of four four-line stanzas. The musical 4/4 signature, or common time, provides a structural evenness that permits thematic wildness and rapid shifts in tone: like a commonplace book, *Talking Dirty to the Gods* is crammed with characters, notations, stories, odes, pleas, and rants that together suggest both the coarseness of human nature and the refinement of the poet's language. Some of the poems are rhymed and metered, while others use accentual measures.

The poems in *Talking Dirty to the Gods* are not divided into sections. Instead they sweep across the reader like waves, with time to come up for air only between poems. The first poem is "Hearsay," and the last is "Heresy": by that one missing letter, the poet signals the subversive power of his making, his rebellion against religion and the status quo:

No, it wasn't the penis

Pharisees wished abridged
& amputated. That season
Tongues rotted like fat figs
On broken branches. Pelagian wit

Could cost a man his head.
Women were already banished
From the pulpit, & their songs
Held only an after-scent of myrrh.

Some sculpted lies & dripped gold
Into them. Others saw burning pyres
& said Free Will couldn't live
In a doll's body, termites in the godhead.[22]

Just as the Briton Pelagius dared to challenge the doctrine of original sin, the poet here uses his Anglo-Saxon tongue and challenges the centrality of the Phallus. Faced with the rigid heterodoxy of religion, patriarchy, and language, some women subvert from within by "sculpt[ing] lies" and "drip[ping] gold into them." Others reject the paradigm entirely. In his last poem, the poet aligns himself with the female, evoking the Nietzschean parallel between subversion, art, and the feminine—the poems themselves become "termites in the godhead," chewing away at the foundations of Western society. This poem's dynamic blend of modesty (termites are small) and pride (they can take down houses) mirrors the book's strategy: 132 small poems can add up to a lot of destruction—and a lot of pleasure for the reader.

Books carry their readers lightly or ploddingly. Just as line or stanza breaks create energy and conflict in individual poems, juxtapositions in a collection can surprise, creating energy and movement, beginning to end. As we approach the book of poems, looking for a text of "bliss," we might keep in mind Roland Barthes' description: a text of bliss "granulates, crackles, caresses, grates, cuts, and comes." Notice the verbs of movement and friction. In order to create a free flow of energy through a book, the poet must use convention, but at the same time must not *be* used *by* convention. The poet clears the clutter and makes the space inviting, always aware that to dictate the path entirely is to block the reader from a sense of discovery. Poets who trust their readers are able to make the structure of the book a partnership—an invitation to find bliss.

## Notes

1. Neil Fraistat, ed., *Poems in Their Place: The Intertextuality and Order of Poetic Collections* (Chapel Hill: University of North Carolina Press, 1986), 3.

2. Marjorie Perloff, "The Two Ariels: The (Re)Making of the Sylvia Plath Canon," *American Poetry Review* 13, no. 6 (November–December 1984), 10–18.

3. M. L. Rosenthal and Sally Gall, *The Modern Poetic Sequence: The Genius of Modern Poetry* (New York: Oxford University Press, 1983), 3.

4. Rosenthal and Gall, *The Modern Poetic Sequence*, 11.

5. Roland Barthes, *S/Z*, trans. Richard Miller (New York: Hill & Wang, 1974), 4.

6. Barthes, *S/Z*, 5.

7. Roland Barthes, *The Pleasure of the Text*, trans. Richard Miller (New York: Hill & Wang, 1975), 14.

8. Barthes, *S/Z*, 5.

9. Barthes, *S/Z*, 5.

10. Barbara Herrnstein-Smith, *Poetic Closure: A Study of How Poems End* (Chicago: University of Chicago Press, 1971), 238.

11. Herrnstein-Smith, *Poetic Closure*, 241.

12. Lyn Hejinian, "Against Closure," in *Postmodern Poetry: A Norton Anthology*, ed. Paul Hoover (New York: Norton, 1994), 653.

13. Eleanor Elson Heginbotham, *Reading the Fascicles of Emily Dickinson* (Columbus: Ohio State University Press, 2003), 113.

14. Elaine Terranova, e-mail message to Natasha Sajé.

15. Heginbotham, *Reading the Fascicles*, 113.

16. Stanley Fish, *Is There a Text in This Class? The Authority of Interpretive Communities* (Cambridge: Harvard University Press, 1982).

17. Hernstein-Smith, *Poetic Closure*, 262.

18. Heginbotham, *Reading the Fascicles*, 271.

19. C. D. Wright, *Tremble* (New York: Ecco, 1996), 59. Reprinted with permission by the author.

20. Richard Badenhausen, *T. S. Eliot and the Art of Collaboration* (Cambridge: Cambridge University Press, 2005), 76.

21. Jorie Graham, "Prayer," in *Never* (New York: HarperCollins, 2002), 111.

22. Yusef Komunyakaa, *Talking Dirty to the Gods* (New York: Farrar, Straus and Giroux, 2000), 134.

# Performance of the Lyric "I"

> A successful work of art is not one which resolves contra-
> dictions in a spurious harmony, but one which expresses
> the idea of harmony negatively by embodying the con-
> tradictions, pure and uncompromised, in its innermost
> structure.
> —Theodor Adorno[1]

I once polled my poet friends, asking if they remembered the
first poetry reading they attended. Karen Garthe remembers
hearing Robert Creeley at Goucher College when she was a high
school student, deciding then and there that she wanted to write
poems herself. Another friend recalls being struck by Galway Kin-
nell's deep voice and good looks. The first poet I heard read was
Robert Lowell, at the University of Virginia in the fall of 1973;
I can't remember what he read, but I can still see his tall form
being helped to the podium by my professor. I remember, too,
his voice, and my sense that this was something special, a perfor-
mance that could never again be repeated because of its unique
time and place. This was an art form I didn't know: not theater,
not concert, but something wonderful containing elements of
both. For young lovers of words, a poetry reading might be the
first time that the art is both powerful and embodied.

Poetry readings are performances that are often not recog-
nized as such, and they are full of contradictions. My focus is
on the "lyric I," poets who read or recite from memory *their own
printed work*, and the ramifications of those live performances.
Although I am not focusing on poets who write primarily for the
ear and the stage ("slam poets"), or on Poetry Out Loud, the
national program that since 2006 has coached high school stu-
dents to perform the work of published poets, these two venues

173

do provide insights into what makes a good performance, which is also part of my analysis.

In ancient Greece and medieval Europe, the oral performance of poems—primarily epics—connected groups of listeners by offering a new, shared experience. Moreover, speech was deemed more trustworthy than writing because of the presence of a physical body. Centuries later, the eighteenth-century American insistence on truth in public speaking and the accompanying class and gender tensions resulting from a culture where a broader swath of people are orators are described by Jay Fliegelman in *Declaring Independence: Jefferson, Natural Language, and the Culture of Performance*. This period saw a shift from stylized to more naturalistic delivery, leading public speakers such as historian Edward Gibbon to say, "I dreaded exposing myself."[2] Fliegelman points out that men as well as women were well aware of the risk of public exposure, that "in Latin, *publicus* signifies a public man or magistrate, *publica* a public woman or prostitute."[3] While we—in the United States at least—have come a long way in diminishing the negative consequences when women engage in public display, I'm interested in how poetry readings are evaluated as performances, and I wonder if a trace of shame lingers.

Even after print technology transformed reading into a private experience and the novel became the dominant genre, reading texts aloud (both prose and poetry) remained a communal, social experience. But after World War I reading aloud declined, Peter Middleton points out, as new technologies such as film and later, television, offered more exciting entertainments.[4]

In the mid-twentieth century, reading aloud reappeared, this time with an emphasis on the author himself or herself. Donald Hall notes that in the nineteenth and early twentieth centuries, poets such as Walt Whitman lectured but rarely read their own poems; however, in the 1920s and 1930s poets such as Vachel Lindsay, Carl Sandburg, and Robert Frost traveled across the United States performing their poems. In 1921 William Carlos Williams had an unsuccessful reading of *Kora in Hell*. In 1943 Wallace Stevens pronounced, "I am not a troubadour" and refused to perform.[5] Gertrude Stein considered her lecture tour in the forties—one that made her a celebrity—as a chance to explain the poems that baffled readers. Also in the forties, Dylan Thomas' U.S. tour became the emblem of "both excellence and the freak show."[6]

The fifties, Donald Hall remembers, proved a booming decade for poetry readings. The popularity of live readings, Hall argues, played a role in poets writing for the platform—making more accessible poems, usually lighter in tone, that is, "crowd pleasers." Hall may well be right, because hearing a poem and reading it on the page are entirely different experiences. Embodied text has different goals from the written text, something that Diana Taylor notes[7] and most poets instinctively know. In a live reading, the poet's body language can assist (or hinder) communicating the poem. Tony Hoagland writes,

> For a poem to be recited to a living audience is its big break in show business. A poem in the air is not the same poem as it was on the page—the drama and charm of its unfolding is completely, particularly alive and intimate as it passes from one body into another. And the excitement of hearing a good poem in such a way is like a rollercoaster ride—I can't wait to see what is going to happen next.[8]

Many people find it difficult to comprehend complex oral language, especially when they only hear it once. Oral performance can enhance, complicate, or distract from the text. When a poet reads an apparently autobiographical poem in front of a live audience, the speaking body can even contradict the text, producing a work of art more interesting than the printed text. Indeed, Shoshana Felman argues that the speaking body is a "scandal" because its speech cannot be controlled by intention.[9] Training in theater or in public speaking can counter this lack of control, but training is never entirely successful. This tension between the text and the body is part of what makes poetry readings into that "rollercoaster ride" Hoagland describes. Today, live readings also take place in a fabulous array of venues, from the concert hall with perfect acoustics to the coffee shop with the cappuccino machine in the background. No live reading is exactly like another, and that is part of its charm.

# The Lyric

In my essay on narrative, I argued that the term "narrative" has been misused for ideological purposes. "Lyric" is also maligned, most often to protest the authority of the lyric voice. The lyric is usually defined as a brief poem based on the emotion of one speaker. For example, Robert Frost writes, "a poem . . . begins as a lump in the throat, a sense of wrong, a homesickness, a lovesickness. . . . It finds the thought and the thought finds the words."[10] Some scholars and poets resist the lyric because of its associations with late Romantic ideas about the self, notably the idea that an individual can be extricated from the culture that created him and that the solitary, embodied voice transmits "truth." Mark Jeffreys argues that lyric texts are "not inevitably representative of a specific ideology" and points out that "lyric did not conquer poetry: poetry was reduced to lyric. Lyric became the dominant form of poetry only as poetry's authority was reduced to the cramped margins of culture. . . . Poetry was pushed into a lyric ghetto because prose fiction became the presumptive vehicle for narrative literature."[11]

Helen Vendler writes that "a lyric poem is a script for performance by its reader. It is, then, the most intimate of genres, constructing a twinship between writer and reader" in which "the words of the speaker become my own words" and there is an "imaginative transformation of self."[12] I am interested in the how the privacy, internal monologue, and "here and now–ness" of the lyric poem[13] are transformed when they are performed by the poet himself or herself. This transformation, along with postmodern insights on selfhood and emotional expression, are the core of my inquiry here.

Academics prefer difficult texts because of the work they inspire, and thus, part of the postmodern discomfort with the lyric mode rests in its perceived ease. In a review essay on the "lyric predicament," critic and poet Calvin Bedient writes, "All the thinkers about modern poetry who matter to me regard it as, at the least, a practice of social alienation."[14] Postmodern writer David Antin, known for his "talk poems" extemporaneously performed, articulates his own discomfort with the lyric "I" by distinguishing himself from its most famous practitioners:

. . i had always had mixed feelings
about being considered a poet     if robert lowell is a
poet i dont want to be a poet      if robert frost was a
poet i dont want to be a poet    if socrates was a poet
ill consider it[15]

Interestingly, while Antin's other writings suggest that he prefers open-ended philosophy and social inquiry to personal expression, the structure of his work, including the snippet above and its apparently autobiographical "I," manages to both establish personhood and surround it with irony. Similarly and more recently, Olena Kalytiak Davis' poem "The Lyric 'I' Drives to Pick up Her Children from School: A Poem in the Postconfessional Mode"[16] is soaked in irony, despite or because of its autobiographical detail. She lays bare her longing to be a poet "like Robert Lowell," (a postmodern gesture that in fact moves her closer to being a poet like David Antin,) while at the same time picking up her children from school, considering her sexual and romantic relationships, and struggling with Alaskan weather. Davis knows the critique that will be measured against her (she *is not* Robert Lowell) and playfully rebuts it. The juxtaposition of high art and the domestic creates yet another layer of irony, one that inflects the poem with insights about gender. A male poet, simply by virtue of his gender, has an easier time being "like Robert Lowell" than a female poet. Ira Sadoff has analyzed the poem's doubleness,[17] so I would merely like to suggest that the poem gains power when recited by the poet because the audience responds to the changing emotions she interprets and embodies. Moreover, these emotions—pride, anger, ambition, despair, and joy—are a sign of the intimacy the audience craves. For instance, Becca Klaver's blog describes a Davis reading wherein "the benefactresses were stiff-faced, but the rest of us were laughing pretty hard. It's not this often that a poet is so present with her audience, present in a way that lets it all in: talking as if to her friends because half the time she was talking to her friends in the audience. Hear it all— and some of her best poems, too."[18] The phrase "so present with her audience, present in a way that lets it all in" refers, I believe, to the interpretation of emotions in the poem and points to Davis' performance of the self in her text.

177

That representation *is* creation is a standard argument of postmodern theory and science. In other words, saying or doing something makes it real; even "faking" something means enacting it. This is not just "mind over matter"; rather, it is "mind = matter." Neurologists have discovered that changing the body changes the mind: for example, when frown muscles are disabled by Botox injections, the recipient feels less stress. As Pierre Bourdieu puts it, "The body believes in what it plays at; it weeps if it mimes grief. It does not represent what it performs, it does not memorize the past, it enacts the past, bringing it back to life."[19]

Personal testimony is powerful. Combined with a physical body, it is even more powerful. At an AA meeting, it can convince an alcoholic to become sober; at a trial, it can convince a jury of someone's guilt or innocence; at a poetry reading, it can change the way the audience feels about a subject. Yet testimony in a lyric poem—even from such socially committed poets as Adrienne Rich and Jimmy Santiago Baca—is understood to be art and therefore different from legal and other kinds of testimony. I am thinking of Nick Flynn's "redacted" poetic versions of Abu Ghraib testimonies, published in the *American Poetry Review* in 2010, and accompanied by the full transcripts. The prose text seems to me to have more authority than the poems. The power of memoir—and our culture's hunger for it—is lodged in part in the very fact that the speaker survived to tell the tale, which underscores human resilience. Readers of memoir also depend on factual accuracy to the point of law, at least for those details that *can* be verified, for example the cases of Nasdijj and James Frey. Even though the "facts" of history are contextual, as historian Hayden White and others after him have shown, cultures tend to agree on which facts matter.[20]

The difference between personal legal testimony such as that given by prisoners at Abu Ghraib and poetry lies in the latter's fictional aspect, providing immense freedom of speech and thought. Poets are free to create characters and situations just as fiction writers are. Some theorists, for example Amittai Avivram, argue that because poems are always a work of the imagination, they are always "fiction."[21] This Aristotelian line of thought proceeds from the assumption that imaginative work cannot be true and from Aristotle's distinction between history (true) and poesis (imaginative writing). Conversely, John Sallis notes that Kant believed poetry "to expand and fortify the mind, rising aesthetically to ideas," while "oratory is cast as an art of deceiving by means of beautiful illusion."[22] In the *Critique of Judgment*, Kant writes, "In poetry everything proceeds with honesty and sincerity. It informs us that it wishes to engage in mere entertaining play with the imagination, namely, one that harmonizes in form with the laws of understanding."[23] This definition is like Marianne Moore's definition of poetry as an "imaginary garden with real toads." Yet her protégé Elizabeth Bishop insisted, "I always tell the truth in my poems. With 'The Fish' that's exactly how it happened."[24] This suggests that for Bishop, poetry is nonfiction and the "garden" is not imaginary.

Other poets have a less romantic notion of the poet's imagination and powers. In his poem "Sporting Life,"[25] Jack Spicer writes, "The poet is a radio. The poet is a liar. The poet is a // counterpunching radio." Calling a poet a radio suggests that the individual poet is responsible for the transmission of language, but is not in control of it. In other words, language is owned by ideology, by the culture at large, and individuals have little power over or in it. However, when Spicer follows this line with the "poet is a liar" and "the poet is a counterpunching radio," he suggests that the poet *can* respond to ideology by proffering instead his or her own version of the news, a version that is funneled through a critical—and embodied—self.

The philosopher Ludwig Wittgenstein argues that "the importance of a true confession does not reside in its being a correct and certain report of a process. It resides rather in the unique circumstances whose truth is guaranteed by the special criteria of *truthfulness*."[26] A poetry reading might be one of those particular circumstances whose truth is guaranteed by the special criteria of the speaking body. The way the poet introduces the poem tells us if we should interpret it as autobiography. The poetry reading is *not* a pseudoperformance, defined by John Searle as an event that everyone knows is performative and thus exempt from expectations of fact. Metonymy in poems, a sign of their anchors in history, is once again prevalent. We allow or even expect poets to create the imaginary circumstances that prompt their speech, yet we also expect them to get the facts—

dates, place-names, history—right. Interestingly, the protective cloak of the imaginary is largely restricted to personhood.

One fascinating example of the divide between the imaginary persona and living author is created in C. Dale Young's 2011 book of poems, *Torn*. We are used to legalistic texts that try to prevent litigation. Young's book carries a note on the copyright page: "This is a work of fiction. Names, characters, places and incidents are either the product of the author's imagination or are used fictitiously. Any resemblance to actual persons, living or dead, is entirely coincidental."[27] While I suspect the impetus for this statement comes from the combined factors of Young's other career as a medical doctor, the poems' narratives of medical mishaps, and our litigious society, I have to ask if anyone believes it. Is the resemblance of the speaker in Young's poems to Young "entirely coincidental"? Are poets protecting themselves by calling their work fiction? Interestingly, Young is gay, half Asian and half Latino, and many of his poems address either homosexuality or mixed ethnicity. For example, "Imprimatur" begins, "The ones who paint the word *Latino* on my forehead / think me lazy and careless. The ones who pin / *Asian-American* to my chest consider me a hard worker." In contradiction to the statement on *Torn*'s copyright page, most poets see a link from their lives to their poems.

One performance worth analyzing occurred at the 2011 Associated Writing Programs (AWP) Conference in Washington, DC, when African American poet Claudia Rankine used most of her allotted time to read a statement of her objections to Tony Hoagland's poem "The Change." Hoagland's poem's racism and sexism (his objectifying female tennis players and animalizing the black woman, for example) might be seen as a deliberate voicing of the white male tribe's usually unspoken opinion (a persona poem, as it were) and, thus, a way of interrogating racism and sexism. But here I would like to use Rankine's response as an example of the tension between the autobiographical and the performative in contemporary American poetry. Half the AWP audience gave Rankine a standing ovation; the other half seemed shocked. The venue was one for the dissemination of art, and Rankine chose to read something clearly not art. Is this because her emotions required a piece of writing that could serve as personal testimony, whereas a poem and its connotation of fiction could not?

Rankine followed her statement with her poem on health care, "Public Option," a poem that attempts to interrogate unequal access to health care based on social class through a plural first person: "We heard health care and we thought public option." Interestingly, Rankine chose to accentuate her personhood in her prose reaction to Hoagland's poem but de-emphasize it in the poem she read. That is, the first-person plural of "Public Option" suggests that the speakers share a common goal with their audience, a very different situation from the confrontational ideological quagmire in Hoagland's poem. Perhaps Rankine read prose testimony, rather than a poetic response, because prose would seem more sincere, more true. Her own books, for example *Don't Let Me Be Lonely: An American Lyric*, include prose, of course. And her prose text on the occasion of AWP underscored her corporeal reality, her presence as a person who could be hurt by words in a work of art. Primarily she was hurt by her former colleague's reaction when she engaged him in discussion of the poem: his response was that the poem was "for white people," not for her, and excused himself from explanation or elaboration. Hoagland stood behind the shield of "art object," while Rankine tried to pierce that shield with her humanity and pain. A month after the conference, Hoagland responded somewhat differently in a "revised response" that appeared on the *Poetry* website, noting the contemporary but often erroneous presumption that poems are in the voice of their authors, and admitting his own racism, sexism, and homophobia, and then noting that

> The poet plays with the devil; that is, she or he traffics in repressed energies. The poet's job is elasticity, mobility of perspective, trouble-making, clowning and truth-telling. Nothing kills the elastic, life-giving spirit of humor more quickly—have you noticed?—than political correctness, with its agendas of rightness, perfection, enforcement, and moral superiority . . .
> I think poems can be too careful.

"Truth-telling" is a key in understanding the debate between Rankine and Hoagland. Jacques Derrida defines truth as a series of shifting veils. Truth is not an entity that can be grasped for once and all time, but is instead ephemeral, changeable, and subjective. Human interactions through verbal and body language are complex. We turn to print and prose when we feel misunderstood.

## Notions of Selfhood

Are we apricots, with a stable core, or onions, with no center? The challenge to the "apricot" model of the self began perhaps, with philosopher David Hume's challenge to the essentialist self: "When I enter most intimately into what I call *myself*, I also stumble on some particular perception or other, of heat or cold, light or shade, love or hatred, pain or pleasure. I can never catch *myself* at any time without a perception."[28] Poststructuralism questions the unified subject, stressing that human beings are never as coherent as we think (or as literary texts make them). Today, every field of science or social science has a theory of the constructed self in opposition to an essentialist self. Linguists are interested in the way language creates the self, narratologists believe that the stories we tell create the self, geneticists look at the way genes create possibility but determine nothing, and so on. In fact, postmodern theory questions the concepts of truth and essential selfhood so energetically and so consistently that there are glimmers of a counterresponse, as in, for instance, Eve Kosofsky Sedgwick's reading of Silvan Tomkins' research on human affect and feeling. Sedgwick, following Tomkins, suggests that shame is one of several inborn human affects.[29] In other words, all human beings are "hardwired" to be shamed by the same kinds of things.

## Identity Politics and Aesthetic Values

Many writers have noted that this assault on the individual speaker, the lyric I, is happening at the same time that new speakers—women and ethnically identified ones—are entering the poetry world. The 1990s, as Coco Fusco notes, saw a backlash against the autobiographical, identity-based art of the 1980s.[30] This occurred, I believe, because in the twenty years before, aesthetic concerns were subjugated to identity politics. The poetry selection in the first edition of the *Heath Anthology of American Literature*, volume 2 (1989), is an example. The editors (scholars eager to reform the canon, rather than poets) chose mostly identity-based work by a variety of minority poets. The lack of literary quality in the poems they chose created an uproar, thousands of letters and complaints about the selection. The political content elicited a response from formalist critics who dominated the critique of contemporary poetry. Would these poems have received such scathing reviews if merely published in journals and books, as most of them previously were? No, it was their anthologizing and the accompanying presumption of the goal of canon reformation that caused the stir. Fusco writes that the postmodern art world is hostile to "the deployment of personal experience as aesthetic or political gesture."[31]

A different example of the treacherous presumption that authors live their work is the case of the poet Red Hawk, a pseudonym for Robert Moore. Would he have been awarded a Hodder fellowship at Princeton University in 1991 if the selection committee hadn't believed he was Native American? Would he have been awarded the fellowship if the application had required a live performance? His career since has been much less distinguished (self-published books, for example) than this fellowship would suggest, and this case points to the need for holistic evaluation of poems, using not just the presumed identity of the author, but also formalist criteria. Leslie Marmon Silko writes, "The reason there is so much strong feeling about non-Indian writers about Indian subjects is because good Indian writers don't get published and bad white writers do." Yet Silko would not deny the right of white writers to treat Indian subjects; in fact, she praises William Heyen's *Crazy Horse in Stillness* as "brilliant."[32] Does it matter that Heyen himself is not Indian? No. Writers must be free to choose their subjects, but their work should be evaluated on the basis of literary quality as well as content. And estimations of literary quality, it must be noted, depend on their era and context, as any reader of lists of Nobel or Pulitzer prizes is aware.

A framework for evaluation that has been immensely helpful to me is M. H. Abrams' four theories of poetry: mimetic (poetry shows us the world); pragmatic (poetry has a social purpose); expressive (poets express emotion); and objective (the poem judged only on the basis of unity, balance, contrast, coherence, etc.—formalist criteria—with no attention to who wrote it or when or why).[33] Until Kant, the objective theory, like the mimetic, was applied only in concert with the other theories. Kant's notion of "beauty without purpose" from his *Critique of Judgment* marks the beginning of artistic judgment separated from other factors such as use or function.[34] By separating what is good from what is beautiful, Kant introduces the notion of disinterestedness, the idea that taste can be exercised "objectively." However, not until the twentieth century did the objective theory of art dominate, finding its fullest articulation in Russian formalism, explication de texte, New Criticism, and often, in the creative writing workshop. When evaluating poems, no one theory should be practiced to the exclusion of the others. Without ancillary attention to formal excellence, the pragmatic theory of art can lead to a misguided sense of social justice, for instance when committees choose work only because of its social content or the writer's minority status. Moreover, values change over time, with one theory or another becoming dominant. Critic Jane Tompkins explains what poststructuralist critics understand—that "literary classics do not withstand change, rather they are always registering, promoting, or retarding alterations in historical conditions as these affect their readers, and especially, members of the literary establishment."[35] That Shakespeare's tragedies were rarely performed for over a hundred years during the eighteenth century suggests they do not have universal and timeless appeal. His sonnets, as Barbara Herrnstein Smith notes, were not admired by many nineteenth-century critics. Herrnstein Smith posits that the academy has remained "beguiled by the humanist's fantasy of transcendence, endurance, and universality," and thus is unable to acknowledge the mutability and diversity of literary values. All value is radically contingent because it is produced within a particular economy."[36]

## Liveness and Performance

The psychoanalyst Jacques Lacan believed that our entry into language creates a division between the "I" who speaks and the "I" represented in discourse. This division is not peculiar to poetry, but rather is represented in all language. The "I" in discourse becomes a substitute for the "I" who speaks. The difference between the conscious self and the represented self is a source of possible change. Academic readers of literature suspect or assume a difference between these two "I's," but other readers may not. And a live poetry reading, wherein the poet stands in front of an audience and reads a poem that seems autobiographical, seems to erase the difference, partly because in order to read it well, the poet has to believe it. A poetry reading is adapted through the human body which speaks its own language, one that psychologists have tried to decode and one that detectives, graphologists, and con men learn. Immediacy makes a poetry reading a particularly complicated performance. In effect, the audience is watching the poet accept or reject—or any number of variants along an emotional line—a former self.

Many poets, for example J. Allyn Rosser, when asked to define the difference between the self represented in their poems and the breathing self (for lack of a better term), say that represented self is smarter and more articulate because she has had more time to revise and rethink before she speaks. She has hindsight *and* foresight—she can manipulate reality to give it an offhanded air, but it's not offhand, of course. That's not to say that she doesn't sometimes allow herself to appear vulnerable or clumsy, only that the appearances of these qualities are more evidence of the poet's manipulation of the reader. If when speaking to you I make a Freudian slip that reveals what I'm really thinking (say "prick" for "pick") or I twist my hair, I'll probably keep those instances of involuntary self-revelation out of my poems. Sometimes I'm surprised by things I didn't intend, but usually, because in my case a poem has been commented on by many readers before it sees print, I've already been made aware of the poem's hitherto hidden resonances. What I may not be able to control is the aggregate impression my poems make. "A poet manifests his personality, first of all, by his choice of subject," writes Wallace Stevens.[37] A portrait of the artist bubbles up from the words, the images, the obsessions, even if the poet uses a persona (John Berryman, Linda Gregg in her Alma poems) or narrates in third person (Adrian Louis).

Guy Debord famously has argued that the more someone spectates, the less he or she lives,[38] while Bertolt Brecht believed that theater could make audiences conscious of social problems and anxious to act on them, creating collective energy. However, whether an audience at a live poetry reading is passive or energized probably depends on the audience member's relationship to the art of writing. The poets I've asked tell me that poetry readings make them want to write—want to talk back, as it were. Jacques Rancière argues that "what human beings contemplate in the spectacle is the activity they have been robbed of; it is their own essence become alien, turned against them, organizing a collective world whose reality is that dispossession."[39] Certainly Rancière's idea resonates in contemplation of reality TV; poetry readings, I believe, are better at creating community and inciting more art—and art usually causes us to question existing values.

Using Walter Benjamin's famous essay "The Work of Art in the Age of Mechanical Reproduction" to theorize about the power of live performance in a "mediatized culture," Philip Auslander argues that "aura, authenticity, and cult value have been definitively routed, even in live performance, the site that once seemed the last refuge of the auratic."[40] While it is true that more and more poetry readings are being recorded and more clips are available on the Internet, I believe that live poetry readings retain auratic value in part because poetry is a marginalized and commercially inconsequential art, one drawing for its audience, mostly other poets.[41] This fact is usually the source of ridicule: that only poets read poetry and go to poetry readings is discussed as a sign of failure of the art to reach more people. Yet I would argue that the intimacy of poetry and poetry readings contributes to their importance, and that the allure of any live performance is due to its uniqueness. In his lecture "The Typewriter Ribbon: Limited Ink (2)," Jacques Derrida said: "Performativity will never be reduced to technical performance. Pure performativity implies the presence of a living being, and of a living being speaking one time only, in its own name, in the first person. And speaking in a manner that is at once spontaneous, intentional, free and irreplaceable."[42]

## What Constitutes a Good Performance

The Poetry Out Loud program offers insight into what constitutes a good performance. Students are judged on their "physical presence": they must be "poised—but not artificially so—projecting ease and confidence by his or her physical presence. . . . A weaker performance may be one in which the student has nervous gestures, appears stiff, or loses eye contact with the audience." Students are also judged on their "voice and articulation," which involves "volume, pace, intonation, rhythm, and proper pronunciation." And on their understanding of the poems, as well as the poems' difficulty: the ideal is "an interpretation that deepens and enlivens the poem. Meaning, messages, allusions, irony, shifts of tone, and other nuances will be captured by the performance. A great performer may even make the audience see a poem in a new way."[43] This is true even when—perhaps especially when—the poet is reading her own work in front of an audience.

Yet John Hollander distinguishes between theater and a recitation: "In reciting a poem aloud, you are not like an actor, coming to understand, and then to feel yourself in a dramatic part, a fictional person. It's rather that you come to understand, and then to be, the voice of the poem itself."[44] Hollander echoes the medieval view that poems themselves have voices—and it provides a correction to simplistic autobiographical interpretation when a poet is reciting his or her own poem.

Poets (should) look at the members of the audience, making eye contact, a connection that is usually deemed important to a successful reading, and is different from the theater norm that maintains the third wall. In the United States, poetry readings take place in relatively intimate venues, seating between ten and five hundred, with the average less than a hundred. Even at the Library of Congress every member of the audience can see the

187

poet, and in convention center venues such as the Associated Writing Programs keynotes, a screen behind the reader projects a close-up. Unlike the football stadium or Madison Square Garden that Rod McKuen, Mahmoud Darwish, or Yevgeny Yevtushenko could once fill, smaller venues make the physical presence of the poet's body, clothes, voice, or mannerisms as interesting as the words the poet reads.

Poetry readings exist on a continuum between theatricality and naturalism, but are always performance because of the audience. Moreover, a reading is always an interpretation of the printed word. The preference for naturalistic performance has grown alongside familiarity with television and cinema. In theater, actors project their voices and exaggerate their movements in order to be heard and seen at the back of the house; on a film or television screen we like getting "up close" and are used to the intimacy of seeing faces and expressions.

Some poets, for instance Lola Haskins, memorize their poems, which enables them to depart from the podium and use their bodies to interpret them. This approach seems more theatrical than reading a printed text. Thomas Lux declaims his poems. More contemporary poets, however, act as if the reading is *not* a performance, creating the intimacy of one person speaking quietly to one other person, albeit with a microphone so 200 people can hear. I once led a poetry performance workshop with poet Linda Aldrich, a graduate student who had been an actor. We paired participants and asked each person to read a poem to the other; the listener raised a finger whenever the reader sounded inauthentic, that is, when the reading turned false or rote. The poets then looked at their poems to see what made them stumble. They stumbled when they hadn't connected to the original emotion of the poem, and their reading was an attempt to deny or obfuscate it. We advised them to read their poems, not as art objects but as natural speech directed to the one person in front of them. Yet of course reading well is a learned skill, just like writing or teaching, and we can't expect poets to read their poems well simply because they wrote them. Indeed, sometimes the contradiction between the self in the poem and the self on the podium is the very thing that causes the reader to stumble.

While there are some training workshops for poets—at a summer writing conference, I took one led by Lee Potts of the University of Colorado, and James Nave offers them around the world—such performance training is not usually included in graduate education whose primary emphasis is on print and/or publication. Actors are trained to interpret the emotion of a text at the same time they perform it through intonation, body language, and pacing, as well as understand the performance to be a different thing from the printed text. Conversely, poets are mostly introverts whose art is solitary; writing is their preferred mode of expression.

Some poets protect themselves from inhabiting their poems by reading badly, unnaturally—for example by putting pauses in places that hinder comprehension. As an undergraduate at the University of Virginia, my poetry teacher was Gregory Orr, someone whose childhood included an accidental shooting of his brother, an amphetamine-addicted father, and the death of his mother. He read his poems in a monotone, imposing an unnatural but regular rhythm. We, his students, read our poems the same way because we didn't realize that his reading grew out of psychological discomfort. Other poets try to convey line breaks when they read, and if the poems are enjambed, this creates pauses at odd places, in addition to natural pauses at periods and other marks of punctuation. Such pacing also reminds audience members of the performativity of the reading and thereby prevents them from losing themselves in the naturalism of the moment and the emotions being evoked. "Performance" suggests artfulness, and might explain why some poets refuse to learn to perform their poems—out of fear that they'll become too slick, too theatrical. A Utah poet known for her performance skill, Melissa Bond notes the importance of practice, yet cautioning, "Do not practice so much that you stop listening. When you stop listening to your own work, the audience will stop listening."[45]

Slips and tics can be part of truth value, while drama coaches call them "energy leaks": scratching one's head or taking too many sips of water allows the energy of the moment to dissipate into an activity that distracts—visually, aurally—from the emotion of the poem. Similarly, it is possible—but not easy—to learn how not to betray one's lies. The TV series *Lie to Me*, based on this premise, suggests a preoccupation with discovering elusive truth, recruiting science to shore up philosophy. Some common "tells" include physical nervousness, placing things between the speaker and audience, garbled syntax, a monotonous tone. Interestingly, some of these same signs of discomfort occur during poetry readings.

Psychological issues are revealed in performance. In a sense, poets who perform first-person poems or even just older poems are asked to act like the younger person they were when they wrote the poem, sometimes an uncomfortable situation as well as one that foregrounds questions of identity. If identity is constructed through experience and narrative like the layers of an onion, then reading old work requires return to another layer, a self that has been outgrown or surpassed. We don't think of ourselves as objects but rather "bump up against our boundaries," as Wittgenstein suggests.[46] The boundaries of the old self are the ones we bump against when reading work that we are disconnected from.

Much contemporary poetry is written in present tense, which heightens the immediacy but creates incongruity when the poet is reading older poems. The poet has to return to a previous state of mind, emotion, and self in order to perform the poem well. The poet can be bored or angry with, embarrassed or shamed by the former self, which then makes reading from that point of view ambivalent or contradictory. Conversely, consider the past tense and detached observer of Elizabeth Bishop's poem "In the Waiting Room," wherein the speaker recalls her seven-year-old self looking at a *National Geographic* magazine in the waiting room of a doctor's office. The reader of this poem does not have to pretend to be seven years old to enter into the emotion of the poem because that emotion is channeled through a mature speaker. The disjunction between past and present probably influences poets' choices of what they read in front of an audience, suggesting also the universal preference for new work. Many poets will read from published books first, and then from unpublished, new work, as if to underscore their continued development or perhaps to alleviate discomfort caused by the old work.

An alert audience member picks up not only moments of discomfort, but the poet's desire to share emotion and to connect with audience members. Melissa Bond stresses the importance of connecting with an audience, which "may mean looking up and connecting eye to eye, but it doesn't have to. You must simply hold the awareness that you are all there together and that you, with your reading, are connecting with each person that is listening." A poetry reading can also charm the audience, which can be linked to the question of status. In *Impro: Improvisation and the Theatre*, drama teacher Keith Johnstone notes that successful interpersonal relations depend on the participants knowing when to raise or lower their status.[47] Poets invited to read are automatically accorded a higher status than most of the audience, although they might (figuratively) bow to other poets or the person who invited them by mentioning him or her by name. Trying to raise their status—for instance by listing their awards or publications—backfires because the position at the podium requires not an additional rise in status but a lowering, in other words, talking *with* rather than *down to* the audience. Similarly, giving "footnotes" for the poems—information that readers might Google if they were reading print—involves a dance of humility: telling an audience what they already know is irritating, while withholding necessary information may prevent understanding of the poems. If poetry is the art of knowing people and language equally well, as Paul Fussell wrote, then the art of reading one's own poems is a magnification of those two skills, a mix of style, habit, and training.

Tone is the speaker's attitude toward the subject. Most poets, when reading, use the same tone that appears in their writing. For instance, Louise Glück is dry and cool, ironic; Kay Ryan is modest and ever so slightly humorous. Sometimes, the poet's reading tone is different from his writing tone: I remember being surprised at Charles Wright's joviality because I think of his poems as serious. Yet they are also filled with aphorisms that suggest a lighter tone, for example, "truth's an indefinite article."[48] All three poets are part of a tradition of Romantic expressivity, but as Jonathan Holden argues, twentieth-century versions of the lyric, including theirs, tend also to contain a critique of the mode—a distance, an irony, a sense of impossibility.[49] Indeed,

191

the performance is another way of incorporating distance and irony, and of embodying the contradictions that Adorno, in the epigraph to this essay, believes necessary to a successful work of art. In any case, the performance integrates the poet's attitude toward the subjects of the poems with his or her attitude toward the audience, an integration that also includes the "patter" that U.S. poets in particular offer between poems. I remember hearing a group of German poets read at the Library of Congress in the early 1980s and being surprised not only at their somber tone, but at their silence between poems. While some U.S. poets also do not introduce poems or talk about them after reading them, most do, and poets can even "spoil" the reading of a poem by foretelling it in prose. The commentary is usually spontaneous (or appears to be): it can function as footnote, introduction, explanation, apology, translation, accommodation, or afterword, and U.S. audiences expect and take pleasure in it. If sometimes the poetry reading approaches stand-up comedy, so be it. This is but one of the possible tones in the performance continuum.

In the larger U.S. culture, poetry matters very little: its readership is small, as are royalties and reading honoraria, except for the vastly famous few. Nonpoets have no idea how difficult an art it is or why it is worth pursuing. It seems elitist, useless, silly. Even poetry scholarship is marginalized, as English departments cut positions for specialists. Yet in an era where more and more art is mediatized, and live theater is losing audiences, the live poetry reading is growing in popularity, and more people are taking up the art partly *because* of these live readings.[50] The voice of the poem may be the voice we most need. "Words / say everything," Robert Creeley writes in his love poem "The Language": "I heard words / and words full / of holes / aching. Speech / is a mouth."[51] His gesture underscores the bodily origin of poetry and its most intimate transmission in performance.

*Notes*

1. Cited in Theodor W. Adorno, *Essays on Music*, selected, with introduction, commentary, and notes by Richard Leppert, trans. Susan H. Gillespie (Berkeley: University of California Press, 2002), 36.

2. Jay Fliegelman, *Declaring Independence: Jefferson, Natural Language, and the Culture of Performance* (Stanford: Stanford University Press, 1993), 114.

3. Fliegelman, *Declaring Independence*, 130.

4. Peter Middleton, *Distant Reading: Performance, Readership and Consumption in Contemporary Poetry* (Tuscaloosa, University of Alabama Press, 2005), 82.

5. Middleton, *Distant Reading*, 84.

6. Donald Hall, "The Poetry Reading: Public Performance/Private Art," *American Scholar* 54 (1984), 65.

7. Diana Taylor, *The Archive and the Repertoire: Performing Cultural Memory in the Americas* (Durham, NC: Duke University Press, 2003).

8. Judge's Guide 2010–2011, *Poetry Out Loud*, 2010, www.poetryoutloud.org.

9. Shoshana Felman, *The Literary Speech Act: Don Juan with J. L. Austin, or Seduction in Two Languages* (Ithaca: Cornell University Press, 1983).

10. Robert Frost, *The Letters of Robert Frost to Louis Untermeyer* (New York: Holt Rinehart, 1963).

11. Mark Jeffreys, "Ideologies of Lyric: A Problem of Genre in Contemporary Anglophone Poetics," *PMLA* 110, no. 2 (March 1995), 196–205.

12. Helen Vendler, *Poems, Poets, Performance: An Introduction and Anthology* (New York: St. Martin's 1997), x.

13. See Vendler, *Poems, Poets, Performance*: "Lyric is the genre of private life; it is what we say to ourselves when we are alone." "It always exists in a particular place—'here'—and a particular time—'now.'" "The diary is the nearest prose equivalent to the lyric, but the diary is seen by the reader as the words of another person, whereas a lyric is meant to be spoken by its reader as if the reader were the one uttering the words" (x).

14. Calvin Bedient, "The Predicament of Modern Poetry: The Lyric at the Pinch-Gate," *Chicago Review* 51–52, no. 4/1 (December 2005), 141.

15. David Antin, *Selected Poems, 1963–1973* (Los Angeles: Sun & Moon Press, 1991), 1.

16. Olena Kalytiak Davis, "The Lyric 'I' Drives to Pick Up Her Children from School: A Poem in the Postconfessional Mode," *Fence* 8, nos. 1–2 (2005), 99–104.

17. Ira Sadoff, *History Matters: Contemporary Poetry and the Margins of American Culture* (Iowa City: University of Iowa Press, 2009), 188–208.

18. Becca Klaver, "Olena Kalytiak Davis Reading," *pomo expo* (blog), February 19, 2012, http://beccaklaver.blogspot.com/2010/02/olena-kalytiak-davis-reading.html.

19. Pierre Bourdieu, *Outline of a Theory of Practice*, trans. Richard Nice (Cambridge: Cambridge University Press, 1977), 73.

20. Hayden White, *Metahistory: The Historical Imagination in Nineteenth-Century Europe* (Baltimore: Johns Hopkins University Press, 1975).

21. www.amittai.com, "The Kinds of Fiction."

22. John Sallis, *Transfigurements: On the True Sense in Art* (Chicago: University of Chicago Press, 2008), 47.

23. Sallis, *Transfigurements*, 47.

24. Cited in Lee Edelman, "The Geography of Gender: Elizabeth Bishop's 'In the Waiting Room,'" *Contemporary Literature* 26, no. 2 (Summer 1985), 180.

25. Jack Spicer, *My Vocabulary Did This to Me: The Collected Poetry of Jack Spicer*, ed. Peter Gizzi (Middletown, CT: Wesleyan University Press, 2010), 374.

26. Ludwig Wittgenstein, *The Wittgenstein Reader*, ed. Anthony Kenny (Oxford: Blackwell, 2006), 203–4.

27. C. Dale Young, *Torn* (New York: Four Ways Books, 2011).

28. David Hume, "A Treatise on Human Nature: Book I Section VI," *Rutgers University*, August 30, 2012, http://andromeda.rutgers.edu/~jlynch/Texts/treatise.html.

29. Eve Kosofsky Sedgwick, *Touching Feeling: Affect, Pedagogy, Performativity* (Durham, NC: Duke University Press, 2003), 93–122.

30. Coco Fusco, *The Bodies That Were Not Ours and Other Writings* (New York: Routledge, 2001).

31. Fusco, *Bodies That Were*, xiv.

32. Leslie Marmon Silko, interview with Christina M. Castro, *University of Arizona Poetry Center, News & Notes* 25, no. 2 (Spring 2000), 1–4.

33. M. H. Abrams, "Theories of Poetry," in *Princeton Encyclopedia of Poetry and Poetics*, ed. Alex Preminger (Princeton: Princeton University Press, 1975), and M. H. Abrams, *The Mirror and the Lamp: Romantic Theory and the Critical Tradition* (New York: Oxford University Press, 1953), 32.

34. Immanuel Kant, *Critique of Judgment*, trans. Werner Pluhar (Indianapolis: Hackett, 1987).

35. Jane Tompkins, *Sensational Designs: The Cultural Work of American Fiction* (New York: Oxford University Press, 1985).

36. Barbara Herrnstein Smith, *Contingencies of Value: Alternative Perspectives for Critical Theory* (Cambridge: Harvard University Press, 1988).

37. Wallace Stevens, *A Necessary Angel: Essays on Reality and the Imagination* (New York: Vintage, 1965), 120.

38. Guy Debord, *The Society of the Spectacle*, trans. Donald Nicholson-Smith (New York: Zone Books, 1994), 23.

39. Jacques Rancière, *The Emancipated Spectator*, trans. Gregory Elliot (New York: Verso, 2009), 7.

40. Philip Auslander, *Liveness: Performance in a Mediatized Culture*, 2nd ed. (New York: Routledge, 2008), 55.

41. Although legal scholar Cheryl Hodgson (in Auslander's *Liveness*, 156) argues that "a performer's interpretation of a text (a song or role) can be isolated from the text itself and deserves recognition as writing," such recognition is rarely—if ever—given to poetry readings.

42. Jacques Derrida, *Without Alibi*, ed. and trans. Peggy Kamuf (Stanford, CA: Stanford University Press, 2002), 74.

43. Derrida, *Without Alibi*.

44. John Hollander, "Committed to Memory," *Poets.org*, August 31, 2012, www.poets.org/viewmedia.php/prmMID/17111.

45. www.uac.org, Utah Arts Council, February 2011 LitOps.

46. Ludwig Wittgenstein, *Notebooks, 1914–1916*, 2nd ed., ed. G. H. von Wright and G. E. M. Anscombe, trans. G. E. M. Anscombe (Chicago: University of Chicago Press, 1979), 79.

47. Keith Johnstone, *Impro: Improvisation and the Theatre* (New York: Routledge, 1987).

48. Charles Wright, "Broken English," in *Chickamauga* (New York: Farrar, Straus and Giroux, 1995), 41.

49. Jonathan Holden, *Style and Authenticity in Postmodern Poetry* (Columbia: University of Missouri Press, 1986).

50. Dorinne Kondo writes that her experience of Asian American theater "touches my life with an empowerment that awakens me to a vision of cultural possibility," in Dorinne Kondo, *About Face: Performing Race in Fashion and Theater* (New York: Routledge, 1997), xii.

51. Robert Creeley, *The Collected Poems of Robert Creeley, 1945–1975* (Berkeley: University of California Press, 1992), 283.